The Compleat Cat

The Compleat Cat

by Joseph R. Spies

Prentice-Hall, Inc., Englewood Cliffs, New Jersey

The Compleat Cat
by Joseph R. Spies

© 1966 by Prentice-Hall, Inc.

Library of Congress Catalog Card Number: 66–24986

Printed in the United States of America

T 15520

Prentice-Hall International, Inc., London
Prentice-Hall of Australia, Pty. Ltd., Sydney
Prentice-Hall of Canada, Ltd., Toronto
Prentice-Hall of India Private Ltd., New Delhi
Prentice-Hall of Japan, Inc., Tokyo

Acknowledgments

I thank the following for permission to quote from their publications:
Alfred A. Knopf, *The Tiger in the House* by Carl Van Vechten.
George G. Harrap & Co., Ltd. and Mrs. W. H. Davies: The poem, *The Cat,* by William H. Davies from *The Collected Poems of William Henry Davies.*
Little Brown & Co.: Photographs of the cover of *The Adventures of Buster Bear* by Thornton W. Burgess.
Popular Photography: Prize-winning photographs by the author in Popular Photography's $25,000 International Contest.
The Cat Fanciers' Association, Inc.: Quotations from Standards of Purebred Cats and The Classification of Cats by permission of Mrs. John Bloom, President and Robert H. Winn, Counsel.
John Westhouse, Ltd. *A Clowder of Cats* by W. S. Scott.

I also thank the following for their help: Cat Fanciers of Washington, Inc. (CFA) for permitting me to photograph cats at their 1960, 1961, and 1962 annual shows; Mrs. Ruth Van Riper and L. S. Van Riper, show manager and floor manager, respectively, at these shows, for advice and encouragement; Mrs. Shirley R. Pfeiffer for counsel in selection of cats at the shows and tactful explanation of the project to exhibitors; Dr. E. J. Coulson and William J. Stein, colleagues at the U.S. Department of Agriculture for assistance in the photography at these shows; the many exhibitors who permitted me to photograph their cats at various cat shows; Mr. and Mrs. Thomas L. Martinke, Mr. and Mrs. Noel Arthur,

Marie Purdy, Mrs. William O'Shea, Mr. and Mrs. John Goodrich for permitting me to photograph cats at their homes; Mr. and Mrs. Owen Pepe, Mr. and Mrs. John Baker and Dr. and Mrs. John Seipel for bringing cats to my home for photographing; Mrs. David Sayre for information about the Abyssinian; Raymond D. Smith, publisher of *Cats Magazine* for constructive criticism and encouragement in reviewing two drafts of the manuscript; Blanche Smith for helpful discussion of standards of pure-bred cats.

And, special acknowledgment to my wife, Renice, for loving management of all of our kittens and cats as well as compassionate regard for the many strays that have crossed our paths.

I am also particularly grateful to Kurt Unkelbach for his contribution to the preparation of this book.

Introduction

Cats are not a minority group. We are thirty million strong, and I speak for my brothers in welcoming you to the pages of THE COMPLEAT CAT. As for people, those who are interested in cats are very interesting people indeed.

That's not an idle judgment, for I have met tens of thousands of people on the way to winning my title of Grand Champion, my American record as Cat Of The Year (*three* times); and my world record of Best In Shows.

There are those who say that I am the greatest cat in history. I find these extremely interesting people.

This book can be faulted only in the respect that the author knows us too well and reveals certain truths that we would rather forget.

We forgive him. What man is perfect?

Shawnee Moonflight
Jeffersontown, Kentucky

Contents

To the memory of
Thornton W. Burgess
whose stories nurtured my early love of animals

The worth of a kitten from the night it is kittened until it shall open its eyes is a legal penny. And from that time until it shall kill mice, two legal pence. And after it shall kill mice, four legal pence. And so it will always remain.

Her tiethi* are to see, to hear, to kill mice, to have her claws entire, to rear and not devour her kittens, and if she be bought and be deficient in any one of these tiethi, let one third of her worth be returned.

*Hywel Dda
Prince of South Wales
A.D. 936*

* qualities

The Compleat Cat

The Eyes Have It

Chapter One

I fell in love with pets when I was a boy.

There may have been lonelier boys in the world, but not in South Dakota. Hunting was a way of life in those days, and neither my contemporaries nor my elders seemed to understand the strange kid who wanted to befriend the wild animals.

Thornton W. Burgess was my mentor and very best friend, but he didn't know it. I read his works as fast as they were published, and all of those writings put together had a great influence on me. They developed my whole attitude toward animals, and I started seeing things, or trying to anyway, from the animals' viewpoints. This in turn matured into a feeling of companionship for all the animals I've ever known.

For the most part, they have been farm animals—domestic animals: no matter how hard a boy tries, gophers and wild rabbits never seem to make satisfactory companions. I never met Mr. Burgess, and never corresponded with him, but I don't think he would have been disappointed to learn that the favorite animal of his most ardent disciple was and remains the domestic cat. Not the rabbit, not the fox, not the field mouse, but Felis catus.

Apart from education, vocation and family, cats have consumed the wakeful hours of my life. And that's not the complete story, for cats have also been a part of my family life and a part of my family's life.

17

For a long time, ever since my sister gave me a box camera on my twelfth birthday, photography posed a threat to my major avocation. The cats were never really in danger though, and finally the day came when the two interests blended. For many years now, as the photographs in this book testify, cats and cameras have been as one with me, although I have always considered the cameras subservient to the cats. I've owned scores of cats and several cameras and have long since lost count of the total number of cat pictures I've taken. Not just a few hundred, but many thousand. Nor do I know the average number of shots it takes to get just the one I want. Sometimes the ratio is five to one, other times fifty to one; but it has never been one to one, and there have been a few times when it has been seventy-five to zero. Photographing cats can test the patience of angels.

What is so fascinating about a cat? Ask a thousand cat lovers and you'll get at least ten thousand answers.

Ask me and I'll tell you that I find everything fascinating: his spirit of independence, his grace, his intelligence and mystic qualities, the sheer ballet of his tail, the meanings of his voices, his methods of silent communication—but first and foremost and above all else, his eyes.

Yes, limit me to just one answer to "What's so fascinating about a cat?" and my ready reply would have to be, "His eyes!"

It is not an original thought: The eyes of the cat have intrigued man for thousands of years:

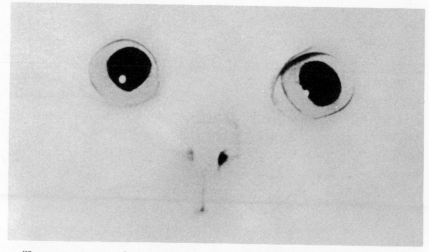

"In most pictures the eyes are emphasized to such an extent that they seem to almost epitomize the cat, but I think his [Louis Wain's] feeling in this matter has been correct; the eyes undoubtedly are the most important single feature of the cat." Carl Van Vechten

"She seemed the Orient Spirit incarnate, lost
In contemplation of the Western Soul!" Sir William Watson

"Glorious eyes that smile and burn,
Golden eyes, love's lustrous meed." Algernon Charles Swinburne

They prowl with velvet paw through the house, like the genius loci, or come and sit down on the table by the writer, keeping his thoughts company, and gazing at him out of the depth of their eyes, dusted with gold, with intelligent tenderness and magical penetration.

. . . . *Theophile Gautier*

Minnaloushe creeps through the grass
Alone, important and wise,
And lifts to the changing moon
His changing eyes.

. . . . *William Butler Yeats*

If all the quotations in praise of the cat's eyes were gathered in one book, I doubt that I could lift it. A great deal of nonsense has been written about those eyes, too. Just to correct some of the misinformation: a cat cannot see in total darkness any more than you or I can; a cat with eyes of unmatched colors is neither blind nor mad.

"Changing eyes" is an apt description, although it does no more than begin to tell the story of the cat's eyes. From morning to noon to night, the eyes change as the pupils contract and expand in relationship to the intensity of light. The pupils are mere slits in blazing sunlight and wide open circles in darkness as they soak in every possible ray of light, including the ultraviolet rays.

They are remarkable eyes. They shine in darkness, for a layer of iridescent cells on the retina reflects even the faintest light. Tapetum lucidum is the shine's designated name, a metallic, yellowish blue or green in color. The retinal rods also contain rhodopsin, a photosensitive chromoprotein (combined with vitamin A) that is sensitive to the purple and violet rays which man cannot distinguish. The net result is a night vision that is vastly superior to man's.

The cat's eyes do not see colors. Man may consider that a glaring deficiency, but the cat can hardly miss what he has never known. And even if we could debate the point with him, he would probably insist that it is more practical to have a third eyelid than color vision. He has such a lid: a thin membrane which can be drawn across the eyeball as a means of protection.

But it's not the unusual aspects of the eyes that I find fascinating, it's what I see in them. Unless the cat himself is being deceptive purposefully, and that's always possible, his eyes will reflect his current mood, thoughts and plans. I sometimes think that they also mirror the shadowy images of prehistoric events—when the cat was around, but not man.

Those eyes have a beauty and serenity of their own. The average man may recall a few women who had beautiful eyes, but the average cat lover can't recall a single cat without beautiful eyes— eyes unadorned, at that. Just as the eyes are unusual, so is the beauty found in those eyes. It has a hypnotic effect, and any doubters should consult their nearest history books, for once upon a time the eyes of a cat moved a whole people.

21

It happened in ancient Egypt over four thousand years ago. The cat wasn't Egypt's only sacred animal (baboons and crocodiles were also highly regarded) but he was chief among them. He was worshipped in the temples, loved and protected in life, and mourned in death. It was a major crime to export him and a capital crime to kill him. The early Egyptians used him to protect their granaries from mice and rats, and they trained him as a retriever for hunting, but most of all he was a religious symbol and represented, along with some deities, everything from life and war to the sun and moon. Some of the deities took the form of the cat. Pasht was one. She was the very popular goddess of life, fecundity, maternity, happiness and pleasure—and she had a cat's head, but was all woman otherwise. When the temple designed in honor of Pasht was uncovered some eighty years ago, so were the bodies of tens of thousands of mummified cats. The discovery verified beyond doubt the fact that early Egyptians properly embalmed their dead cats, swathed them in fine linens, and buried them in mummy cases of bronze or wood, cases that were often lined with gold leaf.

The mummified cats (some are on display at the British Museum) and the bronzes and frescoes of cats dating back to ancient Egypt show that the four-footed objects of all the worship were short in coat and long in leg. Something like today's Abyssinian breed of domestic cat, and reason enough for many Abyssinian fanciers to claim that their breed is a direct link to the world's first pet cats.

It must be admitted that the cat never reached such high estate again. Those were the years of his greatest glory, and in the long run, through no fault of his own, the adulation proved costly. Legend tells us that the Hebrew slaves brought to Egypt soon transferred their hatred from the masters to the cats of the masters—and that's why cats weren't mentioned in the Old Testament. And according to military lore, the Persians ended the siege of Pelusium by threatening to throw live cats over the walls at the defending Egyptians. Reverence for cats proved greater than fear of Persians and the Egyptians surrendered. It was the beginning of the end for Egypt as a world power, and for the cat as a national force.

The eyes of Felis catus did not affect humans on a large scale again until the Middle Ages. Cat historians who think of ancient Egypt as the cat's zenith regard the fifteenth century as the cat's nadir, for it was then that the cat population came closest to extinction. In a sense, it was the fault of a Norse goddess named Freya, who rode around in a chariot drawn by two huge black cats. Freya was adopted by a Teutonic cult which grew in leaps and bounds and spread throughout Northern and Western Europe. The cult's strongest attractions were the orgiastic rites held in honor of Freya, during which many of the participants must have thought they were worshipping Bacchus.

As Freya's popularity grew, so, through association, did the black cat's. Then the roof fell in: Freya had her critics, and they included strong men who felt that the rising tide of worship for her was undermining the very pillars of the established Church. In the late fifteenth century, Popes Sixtus IV and Innocent VIII legalized torture, and witch hunts became the order of the day.

It was a time of mass hysteria, and tens of thousands of humans were arrested for sorcery, and tortured and burned to death. It was not at all difficult to prove witch guilt. Hearsay evidence was often enough, and ownership of a cat was more than enough. Ownership of a black cat was very conclusive evidence, for the eyes of the black ones had the look of the Devil, They were regarded as couriers from Hades.

No one defended the witches, and no one defended the cats. And a cat didn't have to belong to a witch to be tortured to death. Any cat was fair game.

The senseless killing of humans and cats went on for years—hundreds of thousands of humans and millions of cats—and it spread to England and even across the Atlantic. Our own history books seem to neglect the matter these days, but early settlers did punish ladies suspected of witchcraft—and if the lady owned a cat, so much the worse for her and for her cat.

Happily, common sense prevailed and our founding fathers soon rediscovered the cat's worth as a worker on the farm and a pet in

"Here eies glister above measure, especially when a man cometh to see a cat on the sudden, and in the night they can hardly be endured for their flaming aspect." Edward Topsell, 1607

the home. Still, cats haven't always been easily acquired in America —not at a distance from the East Coast, that is. As recently as the gold rush days in California, those who "struck it rich" found it expedient to import their cats from England and the Continent at prices that would be considered fantastic today.

We're a long way from the Middle Ages, but the world is still sprinkled with people who are superstitious about the black cat and consider him unlucky. They say he has the look of the Devil in his eyes. I do not agree. I have seen deviltry in the eyes of many a black cat, but never the pure Devil. Some insist that a black cat's eyes are more fascinating than any other cat's eyes. I do not agree with them either. The eyes of all cats are fascinating, and if the proof is in the pudding, then the pudding will be found on these pages, in the eyes of my cats—cats I have owned and still own (Gooly, Smokey, Foxy, Jigger, Mittens, Phyllis, Hazel, Sputnick and others) captured by the eyes of my cameras.

Of course we'll never really know who is right. Only a cat can judge who is right, and not even a black cat will tell us.

Ask a cat that question, or any question, and chances are he'll look at you for long moments before you read the answer in his eyes. His silent reply will be couched as a question, and a rather humiliating one at that: "Where were you forty million years ago? What took you so long?"

Cats in my Camera

Chapter Two

In this country alone, millions of words on the subject of cats are published every year. The total number of words, however, are probably surpassed by the total number of cat pictures. Certainly, no other pet animal is photographed as much, for almost every American family owns at least one camera, and half the families in America own at least one cat. Fifty million American families, roughly speaking, own thirty million cats, more or less, depending on just which researcher one cares to believe.

The box camera in the hands of a child, and the expensive camera on the tripod of a professional photographer, those cameras and tens of thousands of others, focus on cats every day of the year. Just on a hit-and-miss percentage basis cat lovers and professional photographers should be producing an abundance of excellent cat pictures every twenty-four hours. But this is not the case, and the cats are not at fault. A person skilled in photography should and does produce a technically perfect cat picture, but more often than not the picture lacks quality of expression, and stance, and motion, qualities that impart life to the finished print.

I snapped thousands of cat pictures before realizing that cat photography is a science, as well as an art. Fortunately, it is not a difficult science to learn, but it does require an extraordinary amount of patience and a willingness to grasp the basics of cat psychology. You

26

just cannot plunk a cat down on a box, snap your fingers, get his attention and take a satisfactory picture. You may try, and I wish you well, but I have never known the cat that would pose or perform on command. Nor are cats ever at ease in strange places. They display their true charm in familiar surroundings and in the presence of those they love and trust. Even in their own homes cats will not respond to strangers, unless these strangers understand cats and have taken a fair amount of time getting that point across to the cats.

If all the preceding is true—and if it's not, the adult years of my life have been a grand misadventure—it stands to reason that cats are best photographed in their own homes and by a familiar member of the household. If strangers (from the cat's point of view) insist on being present for the camera session, don't hesitate to invite them for the wrong hour.

Most cats are naturally curious, playful, sensitive and responsive, and successful photography depends on one's ability to make use of those traits. That sounds simple enough, but it becomes immediately complex when one considers the whole truth: most cats have the traits, but each cat manifests those traits in his own idiosyncratic ways. Since successful photography requires the ability to make use of a cat's traits, you must really know your cat subject. Games and situations must be invented to take advantage of his traits. Once amused, the cat forgets his inhibitions and becomes a cooperative model. He will remain cooperative just so long, true to his own whims and not your desires, and it is then that you must get your pictures. Repeat performances of the same game are seldom successful.

While each cat exhibits his basic traits in his own manner and his own good time, the traits vary in proportion with age. At eight weeks, kittens will show extreme interest in a squeaking rubber mouse. Adult cats will be less attracted and old cats are too worldly to acknowledge the silly squeaks with so much as a glance.

As camera subjects, and especially in groups, kittens are ideal. They respond to almost any new noise that does not induce fright. While they become photogenic at about four weeks of age, they are not quite ready then to react to sounds or anything else; only extreme optimists of unlimited patience should attempt to photograph them so young and expect excellent results.

27

While new sounds are often effective in attracting a cat's attention, repeated use of the same sound lessens its effectiveness. A cat's great curiosity can evaporate into complete disinterest in a very few seconds, and a wise photographer keeps a supply of sounds at the ready. One of the pictures found in this chapter was achieved in just that way. In my wisdom, I had a half dozen surefire sounds on hand for that camera session, and I exhausted all of them without arousing the slightest interest from my subject cat. Then a forgotten alarm clock went off, and the cat responded with just the right expression and I had my picture. The shot won a prize, and it should have, for I had spent a great deal of time preparing it, even to the buying of that alarm clock five years before.

One of the easiest poses to achieve, and perhaps that's why we see it so often, is the "kisser." The pose has endless variations: one cat kissing another, a cat smelling a flower, a cat licking a dog's ear. Tuna-fish oil daubed on the subject to be kissed or smelled or licked is the trick here, and any cat with a normal sense of smell makes a willing subject. Catnip is another handy lure, but it must be used with discretion or the cat becomes a wildcat.

At the risk of offending cat lovers here and abroad, I must admit that I find cat yawns almost as interesting as cat eyes. Photographing cat yawns is more art than science and requires an absolute maximum of patience. Kittens are fine models, for they play hard and sleep frequently—as do all growing animals—and a soundly sleeping subject is essential to my system. I place the sleeping kitten on a soft bed in front of the camera and then stand by, waiting for the kitten to awaken. It may be minutes, and it can be hours, but sooner or later the kitten will decide to wake up. The first natural reaction upon awakening is to yawn, and the kitten usually reacts properly and intermittently over a period of several minutes. Thus there is ample time for several pictures, a modest collection of amusing expressions that are often quite human. And since stretching usually follows yawning, a bonus awaits anyone with the patience to outwait cat sleep.

Amateurs and professionals find action shots the most difficult to achieve. Here again, applied cat psychology simplifies the task. Training the cats is not essential and would probably be useless

BEGINNER'S LUCK. This was my first published cat picture—and also my first prize winner! It was taken with a $6.75 reflex camera, hand held, and I used a single flash. Luck was really on my side, for it was only twenty minutes before my model deigned to strike the right pose and expression. Never scold Felis catus. When patience ebbs, put away the camera and try again another day.

anyway. Preparation and an amusing game are the required ingredients, and most of the action pictures seen on these pages were achieved with that formula.

My preparation consists of (1) a prop—often a catnip mouse dangling from the end of a fishing pole, and (2) presetting an area of camera focus. As for the game, that amounts to luring the cat into the area of focus by dragging the mouse along the ground, then jerking it up and out of reach just as the cat is prepared to pounce on it.

I use an electronic flash, and sometimes climb a stepladder (out of camera view) with the fishing pole in one hand and a remote shutter release in the other. Split second timing is important: the shutter must be snapped at the peak of the cat's leap, and the mouse must be out of view.

Sometimes I wonder what strangers think when they see me atop the stepladder, fishpole in hand and cats leaping all around. I hope they think, "The man must be crazy about cats," for that's the truth of the matter.

PLAY BALL! The Arlington Catchalls are coached by my wife, Renice. The team was undefeated during the 1965 and 1966 Neighborhood League seasons. This is my own ball club, although the slant-eyed first basecat's contract is held by a neighbor. The first basecat is Korat, a breed from Thailand that is seldom seen in this country.

Southpaw.

Safe at second.

Good try.

"It's up there somewhere."

Pop fly at first.

"Strike threeee!"

THE DIVE BOMBERS. Mockingbirds and blue jays seem to delight in harrying cats, especially during the nesting season. These photographs are typical of many I snapped during two summers while using the sky as a background for my subject cats. To achieve the desired effect, I posed each cat atop a ten foot stepladder. Birds swooped down from nearby trees to have a go at one particular cat—one of tawny color—and often made contact. The birds paid no attention to me (I was never more than fifteen feet from the ladder) and neither the target cat nor my other cats—blacks, whites and grays—paid any special attention to the feathered dive bombers. Unlike cats, birds have excellent color vision, so their continued dislike of the tawny cat amounted to something more than coincidence. Mrs. Tawny (Simba) has never been a bird hunter, so if there is a moral to the experience, it might be that one should never dress in tawny colors when in the presence of mockingbirds.

WHITE HOUSE CAT. Tom Kitten was the pet of Caroline Kennedy and the first cat to reside in the White House since 1906, when President Theodore Roosevelt's gray, six-toed Slippers helped decide affairs of state. Tom was only a kitten in 1960 when Caroline named him. He lived with her in Georgetown then, and moved with her to the White House following Inauguration Day. Somehow life wasn't the same on Pennsylvania Avenue. Tom Kitten stayed pretty much to himself on the third floor and he complained—according to the Washington Daily News—about "Too much privacy and not enough cats around." Writer Jean Strohl invited me to photograph the White House cat, but before arrangements could be made, a new home had been found for the cat: the Kennedy family had decided that Tom would be happier where life was less hectic. So Tom moved to the home of Mary Gallagher (the First Lady's personal secretary) in Alexandria, Virginia, and it was there that I photographed him. Tom was a blue-gray shorthair with a white locket and topaz eyes. The two little Gallagher boys were his constant companions and he was happy for the rest of his brief life. Cirrhosis of the liver—more common to humans—claimed him in August of 1962. Long before that, I had presented the portrait of Tom Kitten (shown here) to the First Lady. Considering all that has happened since, this comment about Tom (Alexandria *Gazette*, August 22, 1962) is worth remembering:
"Unlike many humans in the same position, he never wrote his memoirs of his days in the White House and never discussed them for quotation, though he was privy to many official secrets."

HOME SWEET HOME. The fields of yesteryear are now dotted with homes and the once quiet avenues are now busy with traffic, so it's no longer practical or safe to permit our cats the freedom of the great outdoors. The shelter for the Spies' cats is L-shaped. It is attached to the garage and has both eastern and southern exposures. The garage serves as a shield against the storms and winds that come from the north and west. The cats' enclosure is six feet high and its sides and top are one-inch, chain link fencing. All in all, it is well over four hundred square feet. Since this is a year-'round shelter, the cats have a two-level, insulated sleeping house that sits atop a picnic table. A heavy canvas stretches from this house across part of the ground area and serves as a ham-mock in summer, a roof in winter, and protection from rain in all seasons. A tree, a bush, a stump, stepladders and benches are there for the cats' exercise and play. They spend their nights in the shelter—warm and content even when the temperature drops below zero. We feed them breakfast in our home and they spend a good part of the day with us.

My particular form of insanity, the hobby of "catography," is common to thousands of cat fanciers, but I think I'm the first cat fancier in the world to push the hobby to the extreme. For many years, my ambition was to photograph all of the breeds and colors of purebred cats in this country. It was a frustrating ambition for a number of reasons. I wanted the best specimens for subjects, and they were scattered all over the country. I had the equipment for taking excellent color shots, but I just couldn't see tossing it into a car, driving a thousand miles, setting up cameras and lights and achieving excellent results. I would be a stranger in the cat's home—and on the other hand, if the cat was brought to me, he would be a stranger in my home. From all I knew of cat psychology, neither system would work.

I finally decided that the ideal base for my operations would be the various cat shows. There I would find the very finest breed specimens, the Champions and Grand Champions, and all in top condition. And just being show cats would make them ideal subjects for my purpose, for all were used to being at ease in strange surroundings and accustomed to being handled by complete strangers—the judges and stewards. Cats conditioned ideally for my camera.

My worries were over—temporarily. What about lighting and backgrounds? Where at a cat show would I find the freedom from distraction so necessary for both the model and the photographer? There were other problems, but those were the major ones.

"It's too bad cat shows don't have a studio on the premises," said my wife on New Year's Eve in 1958.

That remark provided all the inspiration I needed. One hour later it was 1959 and I announced my single resolution for the new year: the creation of a portable cat studio. It took twelve months' spare time to keep that resolution.

So far as I know, the Spies' Portable Cat Studio is unique in all the world. It is my pride and joy, and the fact that it has not been copied by other cat fanciers does not diminish my enthusiasm. I suppose it will never be in production and will never earn a fortune for me, but it has produced the desired results under difficult conditions, as the color shots reproduced in this book will testify. The mountain (of cat shows and catteries) wouldn't come to me, and the portable studio permitted me to go to the mountain.

The portable studio is made of plywood and sits on a base, 2 feet deep and 4 feet wide, which is supported by detachable legs. The plywood doesn't just sit there, of course. It depends on an arrangement of half-inch aluminum rods and connectors for support.

A tough, claw-resistant (but rollable) upholstery material is used to cover the base and as background. The material comes in a wide range of colors, so the color of a cat's coat is never a problem. To avoid shadows, I set up the background twenty inches beyond the base: a custom-made roller curtain, six feet wide.

Lighting is provided by three electronic flashlights, wired to fire synchronously from my camera. The lights are mounted on swivel heads to facilitate precise adjustment, and each light serves a definite purpose.

The portable studio takes two hours to set up and another two to dismantle. It made its debut in February 1960 at the Cat Fanciers of Washington show, Hyattsville, Maryland, where I photographed a score of cats in a two day period. Since then, the studio and I have been in action at many eastern cat shows and in numerous private homes.

It made possible all the color photographs shown in this book, and I wish I'd thought of it twenty years earlier.

Fifty Million Years

Chapter Three

Present forms considered, the cat has been around many millions of years longer than man, and there are those who feel that the cat will be still around after man has disappeared, for the contented cat will adjust to the tomorrows as nimbly as he did to all the yesterdays.

The combined knowledge of archeology, geology and zoology tells us that one of the first carnivores developed on this earth was the Miacis, a long, weasel-like creature who appeared during the Eocene epoch (50 million years ago) and became, in due time, the common ancestor of several families, including dog, weasel, hyena and civet. Our concern is with the civet family, for the cat descended through the civet. It took about ten million years.

It was during this same epoch that the first primates developed —and the primates, of course, were the forerunners of man. Man was a long way off, but both his ancestors and the cat's came into being during the Eocene.

Members of the civet family tree still exist in other parts of the world, and a limb of that tree somehow produced the cat family. By the beginning of Oligocene times, (thirty-six million years ago) the new cat family had evolved into two distinct groups and one of these, Dinictis, was destined to become the direct ancestor of the modern cat. Dinictis was lynx-sized and had catlike teeth, retractable claws

45

Chinese, Ch'ing.

and a small brain. This prehistoric fellow was not brilliant, and he was certainly no match for some of his powerful cousins, including the famed saber-tooth tiger, but changing times proved that he was well built for survival.

Millions of years rolled by, and the descendants of Dinictis prospered. By the "golden age" of mammals, the Miocene epoch, many species of cats inhabited the earth, and some ninety of them were related to today's domestic cat. That was about twenty million years ago, and over thirty-five of those species still exist today.

Man still hadn't arrived, but his ancestors, the primates, were coming down out of the trees and finding themselves well suited to life on the ground. Their strong hindlimbs allowed them to walk upright, they could manipulate exceedingly well with their forelimbs, and their brains were well developed. All in all, the primates were superior to all the other forms of life, including the cat family.

In the last million years of the Stone Age, in the epoch known as Pleistocene, man finally made his appearance. Violent climatic changes were taking place all over the earth. The last of the four great ice sheets retreated some ten thousand years ago and a great many forms of life failed to survive. But man did, and so did two score species of genus Felis, including the species Felis catus, today's domestic cat.

The togetherness of man and cat came about sometime in the past five thousand years. The great authorities can only speculate as to when it all started, and where and why. Nobody knows, but it's reasonable to assume that man took the initiative: wild animals have never been in the habit of domesticating themselves.

Almost everyone knows somebody or has read about somebody who has turned a young, wild animal into a pet. The world's primitive tribes and the aborigines are still doing it today. There's no law against thinking that some child of ancient times found a wild kitten and brought it home and raised it as a pet, and that's how I like to think it all started.

Modern ethologists feel that the society of man and some animals may have been sparked by "imprinting," a behavior pattern of newly born animal life. In the first few hours after birth, the newborn of some species will accept anything that moves as its mother, regardless

47

of the mover's conformation or scent. Thus, during the brief imprinting period, the baby wild animal will accept and follow any human who passes by. For all I know, this may be the case with newly born elephants, but newborn kittens are blind for about ten days and travel only when carried. So the imprinting theory solves nothing when it comes to cats, and is no more helpful than the view of certain zoologists who claim that the cat is still much too independent to be classified as domestic.

If my child/wild-kitten theory is the right one, that was just the first step. Surely it was Felis catus who played the roll of sycophant, and only after he had decided that cultivating man's compatability was worth the effort. The cat took a little longer than the dog making up his mind, forty or fifty thousand years, but in the end he probably decided that free food, shelter and protection represented easy living for a change. Companionship was a bonus. Who could ask for anything more? The dog was doing very nicely with the two-legged creature, so why not the cat?

All known evidence points to the Egypt of five thousand years ago as the site of the first firm relationship between cat and man. And——whence came their domesticated cats? It's believed that they tamed several breeds of native wildcats and that one of them was the African wildcat (F. libyca) which boasts stripes, a ringed tail, and the letter M on the forehead. There are skeptics, of course, who believe that cats were first domesticated in China and India, lands where wildcats also roamed and were presumably domesticated.

Still, no proof exists to indicate that those peoples appreciated, respected, revered and valued the cat to the same degree as the Egyptians. In the land of the Nile, the cat was worshipped even before he became domesticated, and his acceptance, once he was tamed, was overwhelming. Laws protected him and his export was strictly forbidden. Egypt was the world's granary, and even then mice loved grain and cats loved mice. But there were lawbreakers and smugglers in those days, too—seamen perhaps—and the cat started appearing in other corners of the then known world.

Sanskrit writings prove that he was in India over two thousand years ago. Famed Confucius of China owned a beloved cat around 500 B.C. Mohammed (A.D. 567–632) and his followers were cat lovers, and in the same period the Japanese used cats as temple guards to protect sacred manuscripts. There, and all over Persia and in Burma and Siam, Felis catus enjoyed tremendous popularity and was a familiar occupant of the holy buildings, but never again would he enjoy the semi-divine status he had known in Egypt.

Oddly, it took the clever Japanese a very long time to fully appreciate and utilize the cat's greatest talent. They kept most of their cats on leashes until the early seventeenth century, when—by royal decree—all cats were set free so that they could attack the vermin which were wreaking havoc in the silkworm industry. The cats saved the industry—just as they could have saved the crops in Greece centuries earlier, but they never had the chance. For reasons known only to the ancient Greeks, the weasel was rated far superior to the cat as a rat and mouse killer. The rats and mice were thankful, but nobody else.

Did Adam and Eve own a cat? Two world famous artists thought so: Franz Floris and Jan Brueghel. A contented cat is in each of their paintings of the Garden of Eden. Noah's Ark? Some legends insist that a pair of cats led the parade onto the Ark, but none of the legends explain how the cats got along with the pairs of rats and mice.

There's no concrete evidence to prove when and where Felis catus first invaded Europe, but the Etruscans—the highly advanced race that dominated Italy long before the Romans—owned pet cats. And cats were favorites in Switzerland two thousand years or so before the birth of Christ. They were symbols of liberty to the Swiss, and symbols of victory to the Romans.

Wherever the Roman legions went, pet cats went with them. Thus, the Romans introduced the first cats to Britain, where their bones have been found in the ruins of Roman villas; and laws for the protection of Felis catus were enacted as early as the first century. And the Scots became fond of the cat: County Caithness means County of Cats; the Scotch goblin was a cat.

Then came the years of the Middle Ages that all cats and cat lovers would rather forget. A hundred thousand humans accused of witchcraft went to their death in Germany alone, another seventy-five thousand in France, and millions of cats were tortured and burned and destroyed. Of all the countries involved, France carried brutality to the extreme, and on Saints Day, baskets and barrels and sacks of live cats were publicly burned as sacrifices. Louis XIII put an end to it all—but his son, Louis XIV, started it all over again before deciding that father knew best. The terrible practice came to an end in 1648, with son Louis presiding for the last time.

France changed policies in no time at all, and hatred of cats turned into love, so much so that France is credited with reviving modern interest in cats. Leading citizens showed a preference for the long-haired cats and their countrymen followed suit. Interest in breeding cats and finally the showing of cats spread to the rest of the world. By the 1860's, Maine was holding cat shows in conjunction with fairs, and most New England homes sheltered at least one cat. The East was the birthplace of admiration for Felis catus in America, and the skippers who sailed from coastal ports brought home many breeds from distant lands. One popular theory concerning the Maine "coon cat" is that it resulted from a cross of those foreign cats with a small Maine wildcat that has been extinct since 1820. The theory is more rational than most, but no one will ever know the true origin.

England staged its first big cat show in 1871, and it's a wonder that British cat lovers waited that long—it was the Victorian period, and a home without a pet cat was something of a rarity.

All during the past two centuries, literature and the arts have reflected the increasing popularity of domestic cats. Felis catus has won his place in plays, poetry, short stories, music, paintings, sculp-

51

ture, engraving, books, films, comic strips, cartoons, and even ballet. A sampling of famous men and women who have taken pen in hand to write in praise of the cat would have to include Pope Leo XII, Cardinal Richelieu, Victor Hugo, Emile Zola, Dumas, Baudelaire, Edgar Allan Poe, Colette, Florence Nightingale, William Wordsworth, Winston Churchill, T. S. Eliot, Paul Gallico, Izaak Walton, Thomas Gray, Gautier, Taine, Mark Twain, Thomas Fuller, Saki, Compton MacKenzie, Richard Lockridge and Carl Van Vechten.

LITTLE WHITE KITTIES.
INTO MISCHIEF

By Shen Chou, 1494, Ming Dynasty.

Collection of the National Palace Museum, Taipei, Taiwan, Republic of China.

Chinese, 15th Century
Ming.

By Li Ti, 1174, Sung Dynasty.

Collection of the National Palace Museum, Taipei, Taiwan, Republic of China.

Ocelot

Woodcut in Aesop's Fables. By Joh. Zainer, 1475.

The flood of cat literature will continue, and so will the cat myths: there will always be a sailor who thinks a black cat is a sure sign of foul weather ahead, a farmer who is sure of frost tomorrow when his cat turns tail toward the fire and a pessimist who hears a cat singing in the night and thinks that somebody nearby has passed away.

"The harmless necessary cat," wrote Shakespeare, long before Mark Twain penned, "If man could be crossed with the cat, it would improve man but deteriorate the cat."

And the opinions of two ladies are worth remembering, too: Lady Morgan thought a kitten infinitely more amusing than "half the people one is obliged to live with in the world" and Lady Strathmore hoped "never to go to heaven" unless she could meet her own cats there.

We will never know if Lady Strathmore achieved her objective, but we do know, and the knowledge is sorrow to all true cat lovers, that the cat is not mentioned in the Bible. Still, some solace can be derived from these four references to Christ and the cat found in the apocryphal writings of the Gospel of the Holy Twelve:

> And there were in the same cave an ox and a horse and an ass and a sheep, and beneath the manger was a cat with her little ones; and there were doves also overhead; and each had its mate after its kind, the male with the female.

> As Jesus passed through a certain village He saw a crowd of idlers of the baser sort, and they were tormenting a cat which they had found, and shamefully treating it. And Jesus commanded them to desist, and began to reason with them.

> And as Jesus entered into a certain village He saw a young cat which had none to care for her, and she was hungry and cried unto Him; and He took her up, and put her inside His garment, and she lay in His bosom.

> And when He came into the village He set food and drink before the cat, and she ate and drank, and shewed thanks unto Him. And He gave her unto one of His disciples who was a widow, whose name was Lorenza, and she took care of her.

The Cat Fancy

Chapter Four

In a general sense, the American cat fancy consists of all good people who own and love cats, or who don't own them and still love them. The true cat fancier is intensely interested in cats, and he actively demonstrates his interest in ways that prove beyond doubt that he is a felinophile of the highest order. More often than not, he is a breeder or exhibitor, or both, of a certain breed or breeds, and the welfare and betterment of those breeds are among his main purposes in life. He is a hobbyist, amateur or professional. Cats are his hobby, and he would resent being told that he is spending too much time on them. His sincere interest does not lessen his effectiveness as citizen, parent or businessman, and often he will insist that he is a better man because of it.

"Dogs are more essentially the friends of men, and cats may be considered as the chosen allies of womankind," wrote Frances Simpson more than six decades ago. How swiftly times changed. Today women dominate the dog fancy, and men and women are about equal in numbers in the cat fancy. The fancy's men and women come from all walks of life. It is a friendly, democratic, heterogeneous society of people of all ages in all parts of the country. All are experts— in private, at least—and all contribute to the national economy.

No one has ever estimated, and perhaps no one ever can, the millions of dollars spent on cats in a given year in the United States. But anyone interested enough to make the attempt can start with the healthy figure of $150,000,000 which is the absolute minimum spent on cat foods each year, and then go on into such other things as veterinary services and medicines, hotel and motel lodgings, transportation expenses, cat show expenses, accessories and supplies, literature and art, kitten and cat sales, stud services, advertising and promotion, and a host of other areas in which money changes hands because of cats. People by the tens of thousands earn their living, in whole or in part, because of cats.

The power that turns the wheel of the cat fancy is the cat show, which had its origin in England as far back as 1598. In those days, a cat show was sort of an added attraction at a country fair, with prizes awarded on the basis of individual merit: biggest cat, most beautiful cat and best ratter. Country fairs in New England boasted the same type shows a hundred years ago.

Then came 1871 and the world's first "official" cat show, held in London's Crystal Palace. It was a great success and, in the long run, the inspiration for the first proper cat show held in this country at Madison Square Garden in May of 1895. A hundred and seventy-six cats were entered at the show. One of the judges was Dr. R. S. Huidekoper who a year later founded the American Cat Club of New York, the first such club in this country. The club had its troubles and disbanded in 1897, but apparently it lasted long enough for word to reach one of England's leading cat breeders, Lady Marcus Beresford. In 1898, Lady Beresford founded the Cat Club of England. This put England in the cat club lead, but not for long. Mrs. Clinton Locke, the first woman to operate a cattery in the United States (pre-1875) and probably this country's first genuine cat fancier, selected 1899 to found the Beresford Cat Club of Chicago. The club is still in existence and is America's oldest.

Cat fever, so to speak, spread from coast to coast. By 1906, cat shows sponsored by local clubs were being held in San Francisco, Fresno, Los Angeles, Louisville, New York, Detroit, Washington, Rochester, Albany, Chicago, Buffalo, Cleveland, Danbury, Stamford, Milwaukee and Toronto. There were 21,000 spectators at a show held in Portland, Oregon, in 1911.

61

Two cat magazines, *The Cat Journal* and *The Cat Review,* were in circulation. And two national organizations of cat clubs were in action: The American Cat Association came first (1902), then splintered, and from the splint came the Cat Fanciers' Association; both are still in existence and flourishing, and so are several more groups, all with member clubs in various parts of this country and Canada.

Today over three hundred cat clubs serve as the pillars of the nation's cat fancy. A look at the records indicates that cat fanciers are beginning to realize that there is strength in union and that their cats are riding the crest of a new, popular wave.

The CFA, largest of the parent organizations, has added more new cat clubs to its membership list in the past four years than it governed in its first forty years. So the cat fancy isn't standing still here or anywhere else. The curve continues upward in England, Australia, New Zealand, South Africa, France, Denmark, Germany, Switzerland and Japan. No recent word from Russia, rumored home of the first shorthaired blue cats, and no news at all from Red China, where cats were common three thousand years ago and men told the time of day by studying a cat's eyes.

From the purebred cat's point of view, the purpose of a given cat show is to find out if he's the best of his breed present and, if so, whether or not he's better than all the rest and thus Best Cat in Show. He is not concerned with, and doesn't understand the systems devised by humans to make him a Champion or a Grand Champion, or, in the case of neuters, a Premier or a Grand Premier.

The cat fancier understands the rules and regulations, of course, and while he's interested in seeing his own cat win, his interest goes beyond that. The show is his opportunity to compare his cats with others, to assess what's right or wrong with his breeding program, to gain new knowledge and perhaps spread some of his own to others, and then to return home a wiser and often happier man. On another day, at another show, his cats will achieve greater success and he'll return home even more gratified. There were 132 championship cat shows in the 1964–65 season, and many a cat fancier added more than ten thousand miles of wear to his tires.

Photo by the late "Muzzie" of Detroit.

Shawnee Moonflight, a Copper-Eyed White Persian, was chosen Cat of the Year three times. The owner and breeder is Nikki Horner Shuttleworth, Jeffersontown, Kentucky.

Stonybrook Jimmie, a male Persian, Peke-Faced, Red Tabby, is owned by Mrs. Edgar (Margaret) English, Wellsboro, Pennsylvania. Mrs. English is also the breeder.

Silva-Wyte's Ingo of Aldena, a male black Manx, is owned by Mr. and Mrs. Oliver Kayhart, Kinnelon, New Jersey. The breeder is Richard Gebhardt.

Grand Champion Dwendes Red O'Man, a male red Manx, is owned by Mrs. E. L. Schaus, Mansfield, Ohio. Mrs. Schaus is also the breeder.

Grand Champion Revel Chestnut Dream of Hi-Fi, a male Havana Brown, is owned by Mrs. William O'Shea, Vernon, New York.

Grand Champion Addick's Anya of Betty Lou, a female Russian Blue, is owned by Mrs. Betty MacDonald and Mark, Seat Pleasant, Maryland. Mrs. MacDonald is also the breeder.

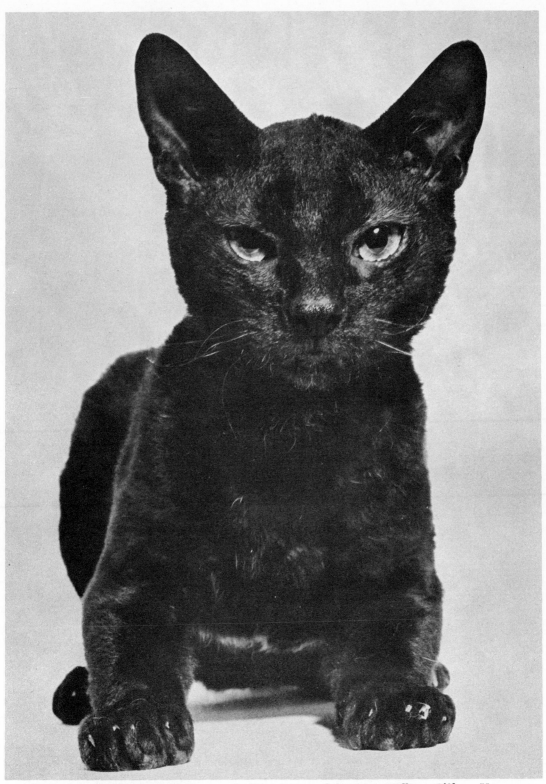

Christopher Columbus of Hi-Fi, a male Rex, is owned by Mrs. William O'Shea, Vernon, New York.

Grand Champion Mizpah's Ferdnand of Brierwood, a male Burmese, is owned by John E. Baker, Pittsburgh, Pennsylvania. The breeder is Vivian E. Chartier.

Grand Champion Chatlaine Al Hakim of Chestermere, a male Himalayan Seal Point, is owned by Dolores and Johnny Goodrich, Vernon, New York.

Grand Champion Your Pet's Moose, a male Persian, Silver Tabby, is owned by Mrs. Dorothy Baker, Canfield, Ohio. Mrs. Baker is also the breeder.

Sweet Talk of Minqua, a female Persian, Shaded Silver, is owned by Mr. and Mrs. Thomas L. Martinke, Newark, Delaware. The breeder is Mrs. Stella Calvert.

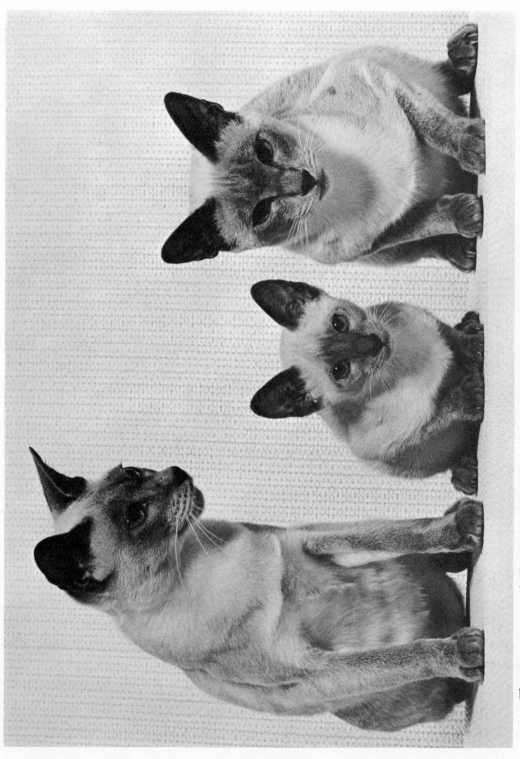

Three generations of Blue Point Siamese. From left to right, Grand Champion Wolfgang Liebsti II of Thani, her daughter Miss Ti-Moon of Jaikat, and grand-daughter. Wolfgang Liebsti is owned by Noel and Helen Arthur of Meadville, Pennsylvania, and the breeder is Harriet Wolfgang. Miss Ti-Moon and her kitten are owned by Ann Ingham Tisdale of Buffalo, New York, and the breeder is Helen Arthur.

Joanne de Ormaille, one of the first Sacred Cats of Burma in the United States is owned by Dr. John H. Siepel, Fairfax, Virginia. The breeder is Julliette Surcel.

Before 1947, the various systems employed by the several parent organizations in determining the relative merits of cats precluded any hope of a firm national rating. Then *Cats Magazine* devised an inter-association scoring system which rated all cats in all shows governed by the national groups here and in Canada. Beginning with the first awards in 1947, then, cats have had what amounts to national championships in each sex: Cat of the Year, and Cat of the Year— Opposite Sex. These are titles the winning cats *do* understand. The 1947–1965 winners are listed in the final chapter of this book where cat fanciers will find the record of Shawnee Moonflight, the only three-time winner and Raymond. Smith's choice as "The greatest show cat yet produced."

In today's world of the cat fancy, the United States and England (fifteen million cats) stand at the head of the list. There's less confusion in England, for it has only one national association: the Governing Council of the Cat Fancy. The Council recognizes over thirty pure breeds of cats, divided into longhaired breeds (more popular than in this country) and shorthaired breeds. And the Council, of course, registers the purebreds, sets the various standards, schedules and supervises the many cat shows (one day events, as opposed to the two-day shows that are usual here), approves of judges, and otherwise devotes itself to the improvement of the breeds and the general welfare of all cats. The governing body dates back to 1910 when it was founded as successor to two rival organizations, the Cat Club and the older (1887) National Cat Club.

The older club was founded by artist Harrison Weir, who had been on hand for the first official cat show ever held in the world (Crystal Palace, London, 1871). Mr. Weir is remembered as the George Washington of the English Cat fancy, and our own George Washington was another Englishman named James T. Hyde. He had attended a Crystal Palace show, too, and organized the first official cat show ever held on this side of the Atlantic (Madison Square Garden, 1895, as noted previously).

The fancy is well organized on the Continent, too, and has its supreme governing body in the Federation Internationale Feline d'Europe (Paris). Cats, cat fanciers and cat clubs are all strong in

Switzerland, France, Holland, Denmark, Norway, Sweden, Austria, Germany and Italy.

South Africa, Australia, Japan and New Zealand are teeming with interest in cats. All clubs in New Zealand are governed by the New Zealand Governing Council of the Cat Fancy.

It could happen here.

Meanwhile, all over the world, the human population isn't the only one that's exploding.

Breeds and Colors

Chapter Five

The whole cat fancy revolves around the purebreds, the true royalty of catdom. In numbers, they constitute the cat population's minority party; not just in this country, but in every land where cats are found. They should and do command a higher price than common, household cats of mixed and unknown pedigrees, for fortunes in time and money are behind all of the royal breeds.

They are the net results of man's ingenuity and knowledge, the science of breeding, the never-ending quest to breed a better cat and then the perfect cat. In his own way, man has been improving on natural selection.

For thousands of years, domesticated cats were spread around the world by man. As those cats mated with native cats, a great variety of mixed breeds developed in many sizes, shapes and colors. All belonged to the single species Felis catus, and their man-directed progeny are today's purebreds. The successful breeding of these aristocrats of catdom was helped immeasurably by three great scientists: Mendel and his theory of inherited characteristics, Galton and his law of ancestral heredity, and H. de Vries and his observations on mutations.

It is the purebred cats who compete for titles and fame at the nation's cat shows. The breeds fall into three major classes, each according to coat: Longhairs, Shorthairs and Rex, this last class referring to a curly or wavy coat. All breeds recognized by the Cat Fanciers' Association are included in the summary that follows, and the standards for all these breeds will be found in the final chapter.

PERSIAN
(Longhair)

Few breeds have evoked as much discussion, debate and speculation, for the origin of longhaired cats remains unknown and the layman often confuses the Persian with the Angora. Once they were distinct, although similar breeds, but the Persian dominated when the two were bred together and today but one breed, the Persian, is recognized. The mystery of true origin may never be solved, but the breed has been known in Europe for centuries. The beautiful coat comes in a variety of colors, and six new ones have been added to the approved list in the past ten years. The Persian is by far the most popular of the longhaired breeds, and is more sedate than any other breed.

HIMALAYAN
(Longhair)

This is the perfect example of man's genius for developing new breeds. Shortly after World War II, Brian A. Stirling-Webb of England and Marguerita Goforth of California launched, unbeknownst to each other, independent breeding programs to develop longhaired cats of Siamese coloring. Both succeeded. The breed is recognized in England as Colourpoint, and here (since 1957) as Himalayan, since its light body and dark points resemble those of the Himalayan rabbit. The breed resembles the Persian in conformation and personality, and its colors are those of the Siamese, plus one of its own.

ABYSSINIAN
(Foreign Shorthair)

The first member of the breed seen in England (1869) was an import from Abyssinia, hence the name. Since it closely resembles the sacred cats of ancient Egypt, authorities feel that the breed descended from either those cats or the wild North African desert cat (Felis libyca). If the desert cat theory is correct, then the Abyssinian is the

79

only domesticated cat with a wild ancestor extant. Despite its somewhat wild look and the ticked coat characteristic of many wild animals (as an aid to camouflage), the breed is gentle and affectionate.
There are fewer than eight hundred in this country, for they are
difficult to breed and produce small, predominately male litters.
Kittens are fragile during the first six weeks, then prove as hardy as
any other breed. They are more fond of water than most cats and
are excellent swimmers. As the purebreds go, they are relatively
small.

SIAMESE
(Foreign Shorthair)

The Royal Cat of Siam, favorite of Siamese royalty, "watch cat" for
priests, and once regarded as sacred, is the most popular of all the
purebreds in the United States. If the government ever issues a cat
stamp, this is the breed it will have to carry. It was introduced in
England in the late nineteenth century and reached this country in
about 1890. Within two decades breeders were paying up to $1,000
for a well-bred Siamese, and today the Siamese accounts for over half
of our purebred registrations. Obviously, the breed must have a
strong, appealing personality, and it does: fastidious, affectionate,
entertaining, sensitive, intelligent and mischievous. It "chats" more
than any other breed, and its voice has a peculiar high pitch, but
who has ever known a perfect cat, or man?

BURMESE
(Foreign Shorthair)

The cat world's only natural brown, the Burmese is royal by environment; down through the centuries this was the pampered, guarded,
revered pet of royalty in Burma. The fancy recognizes 1930 as the
breed's arrival date in this country. The breed has been gaining in
popularity over the past ten years and is regarded as a superb pet,
gentle and playful. Owners consider the breed's personality "dog-
like," in that it loves to take long walks with its master, trains
well to the leash, constantly seeks and grants affection, and guards
its home property. Although known to the western world for over
200 years, the Burmese did not reach England until it was imported

Monk-Chiang Frostee, Siamese, Lilac Point, male.
Owner: Mrs. Sara Reynolds.

Mizpah's Ferdnand of Brierwood, Burmese, male.
Owner: John E. Baker

Ben Mar Minuet, Persian, Cream, female.
Owner: Mr. and Mrs. Ben G. Ehrhardt.

Monkey Biz, Himalayan, Chocolate Point, male.
Owner: Mr. and Mrs. Owen Pepe.

Dabru of Shermain, Abyssinian, male.
Owner: David Bruce McNaughtan.

Minqua's Punxsutawney, Persian, Blue Cream, female.
Owner: Mr. and Mrs. Thomas L. Martinke.

Irene's Laurelle, Persian, Tortoiseshell, female.
Owner: Diane Wilson.

Kalico Kate, American Shorthair Calico, female.
Owner: Mrs. Florence Hamilton.

Addick's Anya of Betty Lou, Russian Blue, female.
Owner: Mrs. Betty MacDonald and Mark.

Caithness Philadelphus, Red Colorpoint, male.
Owner: Dorothy A. Dimock.

Christopher Columbus of Hi-Fi, Rex, male.
Owner: Mrs. William O'Shea.

Miss Hogan's Malteesa, American Shorthair, Blue, female.
Owner: Mrs. Lee Carnahan.

Hi-Fi's Naughty Marietta, Havana Brown, female.
Owner: Mrs. William O'Shea.

Dwendes Red O'Man, Manx, Red, male.
Owner: Mrs. E. L. Schaus.

Van Lynn's Cherokee of Mai-Deen, American Shorthair,
Red Tabby, male.
Owner: Mrs. Helen N. Toal.

Caithness Andrew, Manx, Macherel Tabby, male.
Owner: Dorothy A. Dimock.

from the United States (1947). There it is also enjoying a wave of popularity.

AMERICAN SHORTHAIR

A true American breed descended from the cats brought to these shores by the Puritans. Those early breed members guarded the scarce grains from rodents and were pets in wilderness homes, so today's members have a proud heritage. They haven't changed, and are still loyal, dignified, courageous, intelligent, affectionate companions. Harrison Weir thought that the best ones were among "the most perfect animals ever created." This breed familiar to everyone who has seen more than three cats was called, until recently, the Domestic Shorthair. Detractors often refer to the American Shorthair as "alley cat," but Miss Patricia Barr, a five-year-old friend of mine, prefers "boulevard cat," and so do I.

HAVANA BROWN
(Foreign Shorthair)

The breed's name derives from the tobacco-brown color of its coat. It was developed in England from several breeds, including Siamese and Russian Blue. Shown first in championship class here in 1959, the breed is still a stranger to the general public but it is gaining in popularity. The Havana's rich mahogany-brown coat and chartreuse green eyes give it a striking appearance, and all reports indicate that it makes an ideal pet. Unless you know a breeder, your nearest cat show is the best place to find this newcomer. The Havana Breeders Society has already been formed, so the breed is here to stay, and it's a welcome addition to the purebred ranks.

MANX
(Foreign Shorthair)

This is the tailless cat that crouches and hops in rabbit-like manner. Authorities disagree as to its origin (Isle of Man, Japan, Southern Russia, Southeast Asia, Malayan Archipelago), but the belief that its ancestors included the rabbit is both humbug and a biological impossibility. The Manx is a mutant, difficult to breed, and isn't always tailless: Rumpies, the desired specimens, *are* tailless; Stumpies have

81

tails up to five inches; Longies have normal length tails. In a given litter, all three varieties may occur. It's the most unusual of all the breeds, loves to hunt, makes a fine affectionate companion, has a soft voice, and is a fierce fighter when necessary. Since continued pure breeding (Manx to Manx) eventually produces a lethal factor in kittens, the Manx's survival depends on occasional outcrosses with other breeds.

RUSSIAN BLUE
(Foreign Shorthair)

Russian, because shorthaired blue cats were supposedly brought to England by Russian sailors in the late nineteenth century, and Blue because the coat is solid blue, with the lighter shade preferred. The modern breed is the result of many years of selective breeding in England and in this country. The first breed representatives in the United States—a mother and six kittens—were imported from England in 1907. A few more imports arrived after World War II, but difficulty in maintaining body type, coat texture and color has helped to dampen the enthusiasm of many breeders, and today the Russian Blue is scarce at championship cat shows or anywhere else. A quiet, gentle breed that seems to lack the curiosity of most other cats.

RED COLORPOINT
(Foreign Shorthair)

This postwar breed was developed in the United States and has also been known as the Red Point Siamese, a name that aptly describes the cat, for only its coloration separates the two in the standards. The Red's coat is white and its points are a deep, dense red, and sometimes the coat carries a light tone shading of that red. Again, the Red is difficult to breed, and most cat fanciers classify it as rare. Its personality is similar to that of the Siamese, and there's no reason that it should be otherwise, since that breed is dominant in the Red's immediate ancestry.

REX
(Wavy coated)

Down through cat fancy history, cats have been classed as Longhairs or Shorthairs. Now we have the Rex, a breed with a wavy coat unknown to the domestic cat before 1950. The first on record, a cream male shorthair, was born in England, and the second in Germany. The soft, dense and rather short coat was the result of a mutation, and inbreeding plus selective breeding established the Rex within several years. Today any colored coat can be produced, and the variety of colors may well speed the breed's popularity. And this should be of particular interest to Siamese lovers: a rex-coated Siamese was pictured in *Cats Magazine* (June 1965) and described as having a voice "not Siamese in volume or pitch." The Rex model shown here was a very friendly fellow. The coat has two variations, and like bred to like produces the desired coat in the kittens.

So those are the eleven royal breeds of American catdom and the ones spectators may anticipate seeing at all the championship cat shows held around the nation. They are the breeds recognized by the Cat Fanciers' Association, the largest of the eight governing bodies; a fact worth remembering because the other bodies, between them, recognize those eleven plus additional breeds.

Thus the purebred kitten one buys may or may not be recognized by all of the national groups. If the owner plans to show his cat in competition at the cat shows, the breed not recognized by all the associations is not eligible at all the shows. Aside from that, all the purebreds (recognized by all or any of the associations) make fine companions and pets.

There are those who feel that the American cat fancy should have a single governing body, as in other countries around the world. Short of Supreme Court action, this isn't likely to happen in the near future. Indeed, in view of the cat's surging popularity, just the reverse may prove true and we'll end up with a few more national associations.

A cat doesn't have to be a purebred to be shown at a cat show, by the way. He must be one to be eligible for championship competition, of course, but if he's not a purebred he can still be entered in the Household Pet Class, where entries are judged solely on beauty and condition. So don't let the fact that your pet cat doesn't conform to championship standards keep you from entering him at the cat shows.

Entering one's pet in this class can result in the opening of many doors—doors leading to a new hobby, new friends, the cat fancy and a deeper understanding and appreciation of Felis catus himself. But it should not be regarded as a haphazard undertaking, for the cat one shows should be in the best of health and his coat in the finest, possible condition. Neither state can be achieved without proper diet, care and grooming. And anyone intrigued with the possibilities of this class would do well to keep this in mind: don't feed the cat anything for several hours before the show, and don't feed him at the show until after he has been judged.

Win or lose, the owner will realize at day's end that the Household Pet Class proves the truly democratic spirit of the cat fancy. That will not be news to his cat.

Finally, the shows also feature an Experimental Breed Class. This is for the newly developed breeds, the ones that may become popular in the tomorrows. They exist, they are here, but they still lack official standards and are not yet recognized.

It's doubtful that any of the purebreds—current and future—will cause as much discussion and so many learned essays as the Persian, the longhaired breed that the man in the street still calls the Angora. Back in 1900, one of the great authorities on the two breeds (Helen Winslow) found that the Angora's coat was finer, head smaller, ears bigger, temper more reliable and intelligence keener than the Persian's. To the nonexpert eyes, then, there wasn't much difference between the two. Cross breeding proved the Persian dominant, so we don't have the Angora anymore.

The cat fancy is agreed on all that. Still, longhaired cats have always been great favorites among the Turkish and Armenian peoples, and in Turkey today (Ankara was once called Angora) there are many longhaired cats running around who look for all the world like the Angoras of pre-1900. And every so often, in this country and abroad, rumor has it that a breeder of Persians has a new litter of kittens, and that a couple of the kittens do not have the round head and short muzzle and big, round eyes of the Persian. So perhaps it is still not safe to dismiss the Angora. As with everything else concerning cats, one cannot be absolutely sure.

There are a great many breeds of domestic cats in the world. Nobody knows how many, and here we are, trying to land on the moon.

Every so often, somebody imports a new breed, new to America that is, and we immediately herald it as a rare one. Whether they are really rare or not is unimportant, for they are unusual in this country.

One such rare breed is the unusually beautiful Sacred Cat of Burma known as the Burman. It bears no resemblance to the Burmese, and the indications are that it is a natural breed. Strangely enough, the Burman was "discovered' in Europe, not Burma, by the then (1926) president of the Central Feline Society of Paris, Mme. Marcelle Adam. The breed is now fairly well known in France, and it was from there that Dr. John H. Seipel of Virginia imported (1959) the first Burman to these shores. He was a Seal Point, and his pet name was Waddi. When I first started to photograph the purebred cats of America in my newly designed portable studio back in 1960, Waddi was my first subject. A long coat, Siamese type points, blue eyes, and white tipped paws—that's the Burman.

1959 was an exceptional rare-breed year for America. Mrs. Jean Johnson of Oregon imported the first Korats from Thailand. The arrival of the pair climaxed a dream for Mrs. Johnson, since the Korat is found only on the remote Korat Plateau, and it is considered rare even there. The breed has slanted amber-green eyes, and a solid slate-gray coat with a silvery cast about the feet and legs.

All during any given decade breeders here and abroad are busy developing new man-made breeds. Few will become popular, but those that do will contribute to our growing cat population. We can be reasonably sure that the population won't stand still or decrease, and that there will always be more shorthairs than longhairs.

Even the most avid devotee of the purebreds agree that there are and always will be far more common cats than the grand total of purebreds. There's nothing wrong with the common cat, and usually he's the one advertised as "free to loving home," or the one who costs no more than a dollar in a pet store. He's the one thoughtless people abandon; and then unless some kind soul finds him and gives him a home he joins the legion of strays and ends up in an animal shelter or as another victim on the highway. Alley cat and tiger cat are but two of his familiar names.

More often than not, the pattern of his coat will be "tabby," and the very same pattern is found on many of the purebreds. These tabby markings on our domestic cats, common and purebred, go all the way back to the earliest cats, the ones descended from wild animals. Tabby markings, then, are as old as Felis catus and not likely to ever disappear.

The word "tabby" derives from the Attabbiah district of old Baghdad, where the weavers produced a ribbed silken material called Atabi. The material carried wavy lines and it was nick-named "tabby" in the trade. Hence any cat with lines or markings on its fur was called a tabby cat. The term remains today in reference to the markings on the coat, but not to the absolute color of the coat unless so defined: brown tabby, for example.

The tabby markings come in a variety of colors and two patterns: the mackerel (torquata) and the classic (catus). The mackerel has been established as the original pattern, and was probably the one worn by those first domestic cats back in ancient Egypt, where wild cats with similar markings still roam. The stripes are thin, vertical behind the shoulders and ill-defined toward the tail. The classic evolved from the mackerel and is seen more these days. Its stripes are broad, looped behind the shoulders, and usually three distinct stripes run down the back to the base of the tail. Both patterns can occur in the same litter, but one pattern per kitten and never blended.

On many tabby cats, the stripes on the forehead are arranged to form the letter M. A reminder, perhaps, that Maou was the Egyptian name for the cat. And if we need another reminder that the tabby was the original, we can find it frequently in the longhaired, solid-colored Persians, for their kittens often carry tabby markings that fade away as the coats grow. Many a breeder insists that such kittens mature into superior cats.

The total number of colors carried by the eleven pure breeds is over eighty, and the Persian boasts the most: twenty-six. That total must be considered minimal, for it counts the Rex as one color, whereas the Rex has an indefinite number. Also, although rare, Mackerel Tabbies may come in several colors in the Persian, Manx and American Shorthair breeds. But even in the minimal sense the figure is half-false, for three of the colors, Blue-Cream, Tortoiseshell and Calico, are found only in females.

A very few Blue-Cream males have been born, and most died in kittenhood. And a few male Tortoiseshells and Calicoes have been produced, but most were sterile.

In the history of catdom the record books show fewer than a half dozen Tortoiseshells and Calicoes have matured and sired kittens.

Cats, then, are the only animals walking on four legs that do not share equal color distribution among the sexes. The subnormality, if that's what it is, is the fault of sex-linked coloration, a condition wherein sex and color are linked in the chromosomes of cats and only the females of the specified colors are produced.

In the breedings of cats, like color to like color produces like color, an impossibility, of course, when there are no males around of the colors desired. How, then, are the three specified colors perpetuated? The cat fancy and science (genetics) have combined to continue the three colors, albeit only in the females, and here's how it's done:

*Blue-Cream** (unbrindled patches of blue and cream)

1) Cream male bred to blue female produces blue males and *blue-cream females*.
2) Blue male bred to cream female produces cream males and *blue-cream females*.
3) Cream male bred to blue-cream female produces cream males, blue males, cream females, *blue-cream females*.
4) Blue male bred to blue-cream female produces cream males, blue males, blue females, *blue-cream females*.

*Tortoiseshell** (unbrindled patches of black, red and cream)
1) Black male bred to yellow female produces yellow males and *tortie females*.
2) Yellow male bred to black female produces black males and *tortie females*.
3) Black male bred to tortie female produces black males, yellow males, black females, *tortie females*.
4) Yellow male bred to tortie female produces black males, yellow males, yellow females, *tortie females*.

* From A. C. Jude, Cat Genetics.

87

It should be understood—and most breeders do understand—that while the desired colors can only be produced as specified, none of the specifications work all of the time. The independent nature of Felis catus extends to his color genes.

The third color (Calico) is the most difficult to produce. It's really Tortoiseshell plus the color white, and white is the dominant color of the cat. No other animal on earth is entitled to make that claim. So, with that in mind:

Calico (unbrindled patches of black, red and cream interspersed with white)

> The male must carry dominant white color genes, and if this is true white will show on his coat, the more the better. This male is bred to a Tortoiseshell female produced by any of the breeding combinations for that color. The result *may* or *may not* be one or two Calico females. Other litter members, male and female, will be solid colored in any of the predominate color genes carried by the parents.

Note that the result is qualified. Even mated to a proper white stud, not all Tortoiseshell females will produce Calico female kittens. The chances of a successful breeding are less than fifty percent, and a repeat breeding of a successful mating may prove unsuccessful. A seventeen to one ratio (or one Calico out of seventeen kittens, covering several litters from the same matings, of course) is the best result I have been able to find in Persians.

The continuance of the three colors is a very simple matter, on paper. I have never attempted to achieve any of the three colors, but thousands of breeders have, and the majority were successful until they tried to cross the bridge from Tortoiseshell to Calico.

Still, enough breeders succeed to guarantee the continuance of the Calico. It proves that breeders are a patient lot, and that man's determination is a worthy opponent for the cat's independence.

The Cat

Chapter Six

The average kitten weighs into the world at one-quarter pound. He may be an only son, but chances are greater that he'll have at least one brother and sister. Cat litters average two to four members, although litters up to eight are not unusual and a Siamese litter may number nine. Cat litters are smaller than most canine litters, but there are more cat litters per square mile.

The kitten is blind at birth, and here again the Siamese can be the exception, but his eyes are open by the tenth day and his state of complete helplessness starts to lessen. His mother carries him around in her mouth and nurses him until he's about eight weeks old. He matures in five to eight months. For show purposes, he's considered an adult at eight months, although in some breeds his coat and color won't be in full bloom until he's reached one year.

Felis catus is pretty much the same today as he always has been. One of the smallest members of the cat family, his basic structure remains remarkably similar to that of his big, wild cousins in the Felidae family tree. Any slight changes can be attributed to man's influence.

There's been a big change for the better in his life expectancy, thanks to man. Advances in nutrition, medicine and understanding

89

have pushed his longevity to seventeen years (compared to the American human's seventy) and many individuals improve on that. One of mine reached eighteen years. Several have lived thirty years, and one cat on record lived to the ripe old age of thirty-four.

His coat still thickens in winter and thins in summer, and it still comes long or short, and now wavy, too. His colors, once restricted to the protective browns, grays and blacks that were so important to his survival when the world was a wilder place, now come in greater variety, dictated by man. But the majority of the cats one sees as household pets and strays still carry the colors of old, the tabby pattern of stripes, spots, patches and whirls.

The world is a quieter place because he cannot roar. He purrs, meows, trills, hisses, spits, snarls, growls and screams—but he cannot roar. Only four of his more than thirty-five cousins can: the lion, tiger, leopard and jaguar. Those four have an undeveloped hyoid condition (cartilage-linked bones known as the cranial cornu), although they don't know it and don't care. But the other cousins of the cat can't roar, either: the ocelot, serval, lynx, bobcat, caracal, wild cat and cheetah; and still others who continue to use cat as a surname—fishing cat, marbled cat, spotted cat, jungle cat and sand cat.

Even without the roar, the cat's vocal repertory is impressive. Over a hundred different calls, some students say, and every one of them is expressive. Every sound he makes has meaning. Some cats "talk" more than others, of course, but none are wasters of words.

In the last century and a half, some very famous people have listened with great concentration and learned that the cat's vocabulary contains all the vowels and as many as eleven consonants. I suspect that my own hearing is defective. I've never heard a single feline consonant, but can testify to the existence of tenors and mezzo-sopranos.

I suppose my own favorite sound is everybody else's favorite, too: the purr. It is soft when the cat shows affection, deep and harsh to express pain, and quick and sharp for anxiety. A kitten may purr before its eyes are open, a sure sign that its belly is full. The variety of purrs increases with maturity, and the same goes for the meows and growls and screams, and always each call has a meaning of its own.

They use their voices to talk to each other and they *do* understand each other. The brood queen has a variety of low growls to warn her kittens of danger, or to tell them to remain at her side, or to advise them to go away and stop bothering her. She'll hiss too, but the males are the ones who do the most hissing, and the tone of the hiss denotes welcome, warning, challenge or mere agreement. Both sexes love to caterwaul, and the singing doesn't always mean that they have sex on their minds. A cat will sing to the moon in the same way that a dog will howl to the moon. I don't know what the moon-singing means, nor does anyone else, but completely happy cats sing to the moon, so perhaps they're just enjoying themselves.

The cat is not as independent as he was in the old days, although he's still sufficiently independent for his own needs, as proven by the thousands of strays all over America and the world.

It's not likely that any of those strays wandered around the corner from home and became lost, for the cat's homing instinct is remarkable and every bit the equal of the dog's. Experiments held in this country and abroad have proven this beyond doubt, and those who still doubt have only to follow the nation's press; sooner or later, one will read about a cat who has found his way home after a journey of hundreds of miles. A trip of fifteen-hundred miles in eighteen months was reported ten years ago.

One of my own cats, missing for over five months, turned up at home and acted as if he had never been away. I don't know where

94

he had been, he was not a wanderer and I always assumed that he had been stolen, but from his condition I assumed his trip had been a long one.

Rivers are not obstacles to homeward bound cats. If they can't find a bridge, they'll swim. Cats are fine swimmers (legends to the contrary) and the Abyssinian breed is particularly fond of water.

The cat's dexterity in water and his grace and quick reactions on land can be attributed to the manner of his construction. He enters the world with close to 250 bones, and he departs life with fewer, because some of the bones fuse as time goes on. The bones are con-. trolled by a system of over 500 voluntary muscles, making it possible for him to move almost without thinking. He's an extremely supple animal and especially so with his forelegs. Thanks to a relatively open shoulder joint and a tiny or absent clavicle, his forelegs have great freedom of movement and he can turn them in almost any direction. No other animal on earth is the equal of the cat in twisting, turning and general acrobatics. Never underestimate his artistry as a contortionist.

As a kitten, his teeth number 24. These primaries are replaced by 30 permanent teeth, 16 in the upper jaw, at about six months: Of these permanent teeth, the 4 canines (2 upper, 2 lower) serve for stabbing and tearing of food and the 12 incisors (6 upper, 6 lower) take over the cutting. The upper jaw also boasts 6 premolars and 2 molars, while the lower jaw gets along with 4 premolars and 2 molars. A cat has fewer (2) teeth than a man, but probably uses his more efficiently.

Certainly his tongue is more effective. Its surface is covered with horny, hooked papillae that turn it into a rough file that licks a bone clean and grooms the coat to spotless condition. The tongue is as important to the cat as his whiskers, those long stiff hairs found on the upper lip, on the cheeks and above the upper eyelids. The whiskers are really sensory organs and guide his movements at night. They are responsible, of course, for the myth that a cat can see in total darkness, and for the truth that he's both a nocturnal and diurnal animal.

His tail comes in many styles: long, short, bobbed, kinked or curled. Or it may be completely absent, as in some of the Manx.

If he's not a Manx, chances are that his tail will be 10.5 inches long (9.9 for a female) and that minus the tail his body length will be 20.5 inches (20.1 for a female).

The tail of Felis catus is more than an ornament. It's his balancing agent when he's up high and in a precarious position, and his rudder when he swims. He talks with it, too: swishing it from behind an arched back as a warning to others to keep their distance and not tempt his anger, or waving it slowly from behind an unarched back to advise that he's in the mood for affection. He's indifferent to the world if the tail is carried up and stiff, but he's content and satisfied with all he sees if just the tip of the upright tail curves over. He's thinking and doesn't want to be disturbed when he's just sitting there and the tip of his tail twitches, and the same twitch in a sleeping cat's tail means that he's having pleasant dreams.

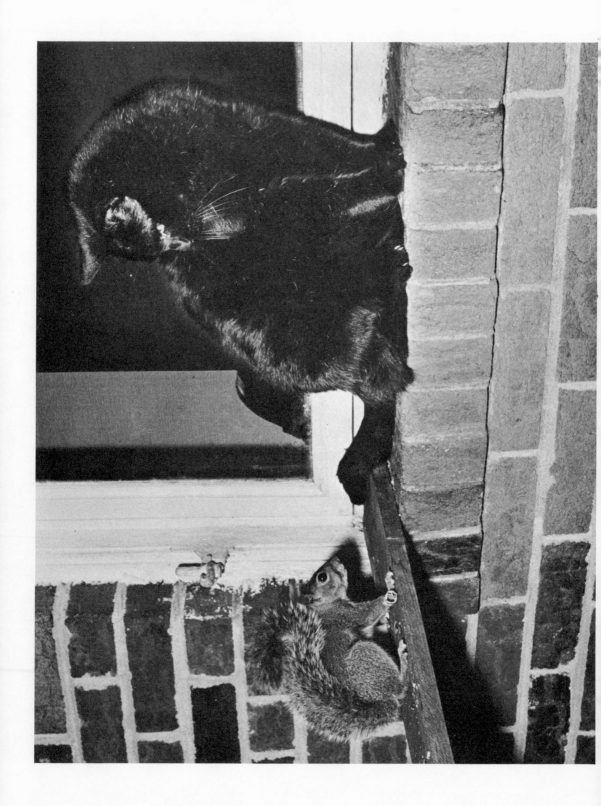

At least one cat authority has come up with an average weight for the average domestic cat: 6.2 pounds (5.4 for a female). The weight of any cat, however, depends on many factors: sex, nutrition, breed, age and degree of activity. Most cats will fall within the range of 5 to 15 pounds, although I once knew one who tipped the scales at 28 pounds.

Regardless of the pounds he packs, the average cat will have a normal body temperature of 101.5° F. He breathes at the rate of 26 times per minute, and starts life at a kitten rate of 300 heartbeats a minute, slowing down to 120 as an adult.

Since cats are carnivorous, meat and fish are their principal foods. But they are not entirely carnivorous, and most have a fondness for vegetables, cooked eggs and cheeses. Contrary to popular opinion, the adult cat does not need milk.

There's no telling what the individual cat will or will not eat. One of mine dotes on puffed rice, and none of the others will touch the stuff. Some cats will turn up their noses at shellfish and others will devour all that is offered them. Tastes run from the common to the bizarre, and many a cat lover claims that his cat will eat anything he does.

For those tempted to experiment and feed their cats tidbits of almost anything, this caution: watch the starches. While the cat's digestive system is like man's, the salivary juices are not. They are deficient in ptyalin, the enzyme which, as every kitten knows, hydrolyzes starches into their component monosaccharidic sugars. In other words, digesting starches is a long, slow process for the cat. But it does not make him feel inferior to man, for his protein-digesting enzymes are vastly superior to man's—so potent that they will soften a bone within an hour.

Among other claims to distinction, Felis catus is the original toe dancer. Walking or running, he moves about on his toes, five toes on each forefoot and four on each hindfoot, if he's a normal cat. Six or seven toes up front and six on the hind feet are not uncommon. If you see a cat with eight toes on one foot, you're looking at a record breaker.

No other animal has the cat's delicate sense of touch. He uses his front paws to examine an object as an artist uses his brush to touch

102

up a painting. His whiskers and his eyebrows are his main organs of touch, but he can also make use of every other hair on his body. He's the safest of all animals to put in a dark china shop.

His hearing is at least equal to the dog's, or very superior to man's, and some recent tests have indicated that he's attuned to higher frequencies than the dog. And he's unique in at least one respect: he's a stranger to motion sickness and usually won't become carsick or seasick. The reason for this still defies the world of science, but it is related to the inner ear, the seat of balance for all animal life. It doesn't help when the cat is falling, he won't always land on his feet.

I would rate the normal cat's sense of hearing as both acute and interpretive, for he soon learns to distinguish his owner's step and even the motor of the family car. Some cats are born deaf, of course, and deafness is commonest among the blue-eyed whites. Science doesn't know why, but inheritance is the likeliest factor, and selective breeding is making progress in eliminating the occurrences.

Deafness does not reduce his value as a pet. His other senses compensate; he lives a more alert life and he lives a full life, if he's not exposed to busy highways. Cat intelligence reaches its zenith in the deaf cat.

One of the most interesting and least known stories to come out of London during World War II concerned the common experiences of many cat fanciers during the long months of the flying bombs. Those bombs were headed for London at a speed of hundreds of miles per hour, and yet minutes before the warning sirens sounded, cats would display signs of nervousness and seek a place to hide. Cat radar was often more efficient than army radar. Many a London cat fancier insists he would not be alive today if it weren't for his cats.

No animal has a better eye for judging distances. He knows just how far he must leap to catch a prey, and just how far he has to jump to reach a limb. If either is beyond his capabilities (in his judgment), he won't even try.

His sense of smell has been underestimated down through the years. He can scent the sex of another cat at quite a distance, and if there's catnip hidden in a drawer he'll know it's there. He's attracted to the delicate scents (flowers and perfumes) much more than dogs are. His sense of scent is far more discriminating than the dog's, and it may be that those unfamiliar with the cat consider the dog's nose keener because the dog always seems to be smelling everything in sight. The wild cousins of Felis catus still follow a spoor as well as any hound.

In a very few words, just what is the cat?

Well, he starts as a kitten, of course, and the average kitten weighs into the world at . . . . . .

Welcome

Chapter Seven

Cats outnumber dogs in the United States, England, Europe, Asia and the world. They outnumber cat owners, too, sad to say, and the proof of that can be found in any animal shelter. The shelters in our big cities are forced to put down tens of thousands of cats each year. New York City alone destroys over a hundred thousand cats yearly.

An animal shelter is a humane place to acquire a kitten or a cat. An expensive place would be a purebred cattery. Between those two extremes, pet stores and friends are common sources. Or, if you happen to be in the right place at the right time, the kitten or cat who will become a part of your life will find you.

It's not likely that the kitten who strays into your life will be a purebred. For those with a purebred on their mind and a willingness to pay for value, the various cat shows are a blessing. Exhibitors frequently bring kittens to cat shows and offer them for sale to interested parties, and often the shows are the only places to find the less popular of the pure breeds. But no matter where one buys a purebred kitten, there are two precautions to observe: (1) obtain the kitten's registration certificate, and (2) purchase only on the condition that the kitten passes a veterinarian's health examination. No reliable breeder will dissent.

Every normal human being deserves the ownership and companionship of Felis catus, but there seem to be three popular reasons that some normal people do not own cats:

1) Somebody in the family is allergic to cats. A valid reason for not owning a cat.

2) There's a baby in the family. It is true that a cat should not be allowed alone with a young child because it may playfully get too close. But the old-wive's tale that a cat will "suck the breath" of a sleeping baby, is nonsense. The informant was probably thinking of a hippopotamus.

3) There's a dog in the family, and all dogs are supposed to hate cats. This is nonsense, too. Unless the dog is vicious, a slow introduction to a kitten is the only requirement. Conversely, a cat will accept a pup. Just don't throw one at the other. An adult dog takes a little longer to accept an adult cat, and an adult cat takes even longer to accept another adult cat.

Aside from allergy, then, there's no reason for a normal person with a home or apartment not to have a cat, if he desires one.

Nine times out of ten, the pet cat is a kitten when he starts living with his new family. If his new owners have any choice in the matter, from eight to twelve weeks is a good age range during which to bring the kitten home, although he shouldn't come home at all, regardless of age, breed or source, if he's not a healthy specimen. One doesn't have to be an expert to judge a kitten's probable state of health, as these few but important points testify:

Nose:	moist and cool to the touch; a runny nose is a sure sign of disease.
Eyes:	bright and clear, not watery.
Ears:	clean and free from ear mites.
Hearing:	head should turn quickly when a sharp noise is made to rear. White kittens are sometimes born deaf.
Mouth:	firm and pink.
Coat:	glossy; bare spots indicate skin infection.
Rear:	check area under tail for signs of diarrhea.
Personality:	lively, playful and aggressive; shy away from the timid ones.

If all those points check out, one can be reasonably sure that the kitten is healthy. The only way to be very sure, of course, is to rush the kitten to a veterinarian; that is a must if the new pet hasn't already been innoculated for feline enteritis, a deadly disease, highly contagious, that can take a kitten's life within a day. Feline enteritis is unrelated to the canine distempers; cats are not susceptible to those dog diseases, and vice-versa.

Health assured, the kitten is ready for his new home. Watching him grow over the months is both a pleasure and a responsibility: it's a joy to watch his antics, but he must be curbed when he performs outrageously. His personality develops rapidly and at about seven months is pretty much set for life. It doesn't take him long to learn the meaning of "No" when the command is repeated and accompanied by a mild corrective measure. The kitten is responsive to the tone of a human voice, and if tone alone won't do the trick then a clap of hands, a slight whack with a rolled newspaper on the quarters, or a tap on the foot pads will.

Some kittens mature into bad actors. They are always less to blame than their more intelligent and careless owners.

Too often insufficient thought is given to the sex of the cat wanted as a pet and not as a mother of kittens or a wanderer in the night. Each sex has one major disadvantage: the male "sprays" and the female has her heat periods.

Spraying is the voluntary discharge of a pungent fluid, almost anywhere and anytime. It's a natural function of the adult male and is his way of warning other males to stay clear of his territory, and it's also his smoke signal to interested females that he's available and willing.

During her heat periods, the female calls out her anxiety to meet gentlemen interested in fatherhood. The adult females can be expected to go through these periods several times a year and are a bit difficult to live with at those times.

As an indoor cat, then, neither male nor female makes an ideal pet. Happily, there is a solution, and it's called neutering: a male is castrated, a female is spayed. This renders the male impotent and puts a stop to his spraying. The neutered female is forevermore incapable of reproduction and loses the inspiration for calling. Neutering is not a home operation. It should be performed by a veterinarian when the cat is about eight months old. It is not dangerous, causes only slight temporary discomfort, and doesn't affect the neutered cat's future except for dismissing any chances for parenthood.

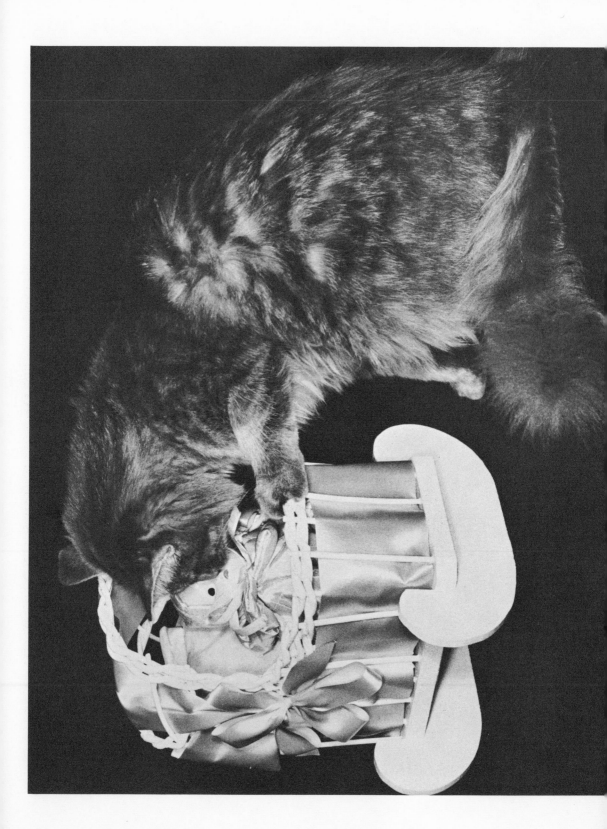

There are those who claim that a neutered cat becomes fat and lazy. Nonsense. A fat cat is always an overfed cat, neutered or not.

Determining the sex of a kitten puzzles many people, for there's nothing obvious about the underdeveloped sex organs. Just lift the tail: the anus and undeveloped organs resemble a colon (:) on the male, an inverted exclamation mark (¡) on the female. Far simpler than sexing a bunny.

Once the matter of desired sex has been decided, there's the little matter of coat: longhair or shorthair? Both types will need grooming if the cats underneath are to stay healthy and look their best. The longhaired breeds require more grooming, of course, and a daily going over should be a must for cats who wander about in the outdoors. The long coats are magnets for burrs, fleas, seeds, bits of bark and dirt.

The tools for grooming are two combs (broad-toothed and fine-toothed) and a stiff brush. Any kind will do, but pet shops carry the special combs and brushes designed for use on Felis catus. There's nothing complex about the grooming operation, and most kitten and cat customers learn to enjoy it: (1) the broad comb is used first, to free the coat of any mats and foreign items; (2) the fine comb is the follow-up, and it removes any loitering fleas; (3) the brush is applied in short, vigorous sweeps against the natural line of the coat, tail to head, so that loose hairs will come free, (4) and then the brush is applied in longer opposite sweeps to restore the natural fall of the coat. All parts of the body should be groomed, and it is never too early to start grooming a longhaired kitten, so that he'll be an old hand at remaining still as an adult.

The grooming of the shorthaired breeds is less time consuming and that's one reason they're so popular. Any shed hairs are less apparent around the house, too.

A kitten old enough to begin life in a new home is still a baby and should be regarded as such. His brain is just beginning to file data and he does not understand English or any other language. Gentle handling is required, his mind can do without fear and his body is not helped by internal injury. Anyone who picks up a kitten (or a cat) by the scruff of the neck or by the tail deserves similar treatment. There's just one proper way to pick up Felis catus: one hand under the chest, the other hand under the hind quarters.

114

Housebreaking the kitten can be a simple matter and usually it is. The comfort station should be a pan or box deep enough to hold litter (commercial litter, sand, sawdust, or shredded newspaper) and should always be placed in the same spot on the floor. The kitten is introduced to his private place by being placed in it frequently, especially when he shows signs of restlessness. Cats are instinctively clean, and kittens demonstrate that instinct early. If the comfort station is cleaned daily, the kitten will have very few accidents, if any.

All cats trim their front claws, and just as surely as the night follows the day the ones destined to live indoors most of the time are going to seek substitutes for the tree trunks they find outdoors. They must scratch on something to trim those claws, and they consider rugs and overstuffed furniture ideal for the purpose. So it's wise to provide the pet cat with an indoor scratch post and to train him to use it. Most pet stores sell them, or they are easy to make. The perfect scratch post is either vertical or at an angle rather than horizontal, to permit stretching as well as scratching, but nobody ever told that to Mark Twain. He designed a footstool which served also as a scratch post for his many cats. The stool consisted of a wooden X-brace on each end, with an oversized rolling pin set by its handles on the braces. The rolling pin was covered with thick rug, and its free handles allowed the pin to turn as the cats scratched. Twain lost fortunes on some of his inventions, but not on his combination footstool. He never put it into production. At least one of those stools is still in his Hartford home, now a museum.

For those who can't be bothered with scratch posts, the pet supply industry offers cat-repellent sprays for application to prized furniture. The sprays are often effective, but I've known cats who found them attractive and clawed away at the furniture anyway.

In the case of the oddball who just won't use a scratch post and refuses to be repelled, clipping the tips of the claws is the answer. Clipping is best started during kittenhood, when the owner of the claws is less likely to object. Once started, the treatment should be repeated every two weeks. A lesson from an experienced clipper is the only training necessary.

Surgical removal of the claws (forefeet only) is considered a last resort by most cat fanciers. The operation guarantees the survival of furniture, but it doesn't help the cat when he's climbing or hunting

115

or defending himself. The claws will not grow in again. Declawing is *not* for the cat who is permitted to run outdoors: it's for the rare individual who lives indoors and just won't respond to training and discipline, and really doesn't need his claws anyway.

No other animal spends as much time grooming himself as the cat. It's an admirable trait, but unfortunately it can result in adversity, for all that licking means the swallowing of some loose hairs and causes hair balls to form in the digestive tract. Doing the grooming for him is the only way to keep the cat from swallowing too many loose hairs. A few minutes of daily grooming with brush and combs suffice, and a healthier, happier, better coated cat results.

Hair balls are one of the reasons the cat, wild or domestic, eats grass. The greens help him regurgitate the troublesome, feltlike rolls that can block his intestines. But grass isn't always available to the city cat, or to other cats in all seasons, and many owners resort to an antidote that does just the opposite of grass: it lubricates the cat's innards and provides easy passage for the balls. This is accomplished by smearing the cat's nose occasionally with plain petroleum jelly (or flavored jelly available at pet stores) which the cat licks off and swallows.

Hair balls are the cat's penalty for being so meticulous about cleanliness. It's ironic, but he's the responsible party. His determination to stay clean makes him an ideal household pet, and the average cat hardly ever needs a bath. Oh, he might fall into something, or something unpleasant might spill on him, but the only tools needed to remedy such accidents are a damp cloth and a brush.

Cats can be trained to collar and leash, but the older the cat, the longer the training period, so it's best to begin with the kitten. There's danger in a collar, however, especially when worn outdoors. The collar can catch on a limb and hang the cat. Those accidents happen often, and sometimes very quickly. Years ago, I watched one of my cats who was wearing a collar with leash attached, escape and climb a tree in the yard. Moments later, as the cat started to descend, the leash caught on a branch and the cat was dangling in space and strangling. A ladder was handy and I rescued the cat; since then no cat of mine has ever run loose wearing a collar. I won't even trust breakaway collars, although they are the lesser of the collar evils.

For those who insist on collars, the type with bell attached may not constitute cruelty, but it does annoy the wearer. The primary purpose of the bell-collar, of course, is to sound a warning to songbirds being stalked by the cat. The purpose is more honorable than effective. A cat determined to hunt birds soon readjusts the timing of his leap and becomes an even more efficient hunter.

While it is true that most cats will hunt songbirds, an instinct that goes all the way back to the wild days, their total destruction of bird life is far less than the cat's detractors would have us believe. A bird is an elusive prey, and the cat, while a contortionist, still cannot fly. If the hunting is fine almost any cat prefers rats, mice, shrews, moles and chipmunks. A bell-collar won't save rats, mice and shrews, either, in case anyone is interested in the preservation of those little fellows.

Hunting is a form of amusement for the pet cat, and he can be trained not to hunt through properly applied and timed punishment. But don't bet on it. Authorities differ as to whether one should or should not punish the adult cat, and I must confess to being somewhere in-between. A corrective tone of voice will work wonders with one cat and fall upon deaf ears with another. A gentle slap over the quarters will keep one cat off a certain chair for the rest of his life, a hundred such slaps will make no impression on a second, and a third might be frightened into complete disobedience. Each cat, each kitten in a given litter, develops his own personality, and sooner or later the wise one learns how to bend that personality to his will. When people speak of training cats, I think of tricking cats. While no other domestic pet is quite as independent in spirit, none of the others are as appreciative of kindness, care and love, or as anxious to cooperate —when in the mood.

No other animal has an equal capacity for self-amusement, either. Any small object that rolls or tumbles or moves is a satisfactory toy for kittens and cats who are great inventors of games. Kittens consider almost anything a toy, and if the object is small enough, the toy often becomes something to eat. So kittens must be supervised: pins, needles, beads, pieces of glass, string and rubber bands are among the items not beneficial to a kitten's diet. Catnip toys bring joy to the gloomiest of cats, but a broken one will scatter the catnip stems used for stuffing and those stems are dangerous for kittens.

117

A cat may look bored, but he's never really bored, for he's one of this world's most inquisitive animals. His quest for knowledge is never ending and leads him into the unlikeliest places: garbage cans, refrigerators, freezers, washing machines, trunks, dryers, ovens, paint cans, motors, fans, drawers and closets. "Check before closing or starting" should be the motto of every cat owner.

Experienced owners consider a cat carrying case a necessity, and in any event it's a great convenience. There are times when the cat must travel, to the veterinarian's or to Aunt Mabel's house, and the case keeps him comfortable, confined and out of danger. Pet stores have the cases in many styles and price ranges. I prefer the fiber cases to the drafty wicker ones.

If that choice sounds finicky, let me add that even a kitten has the brains to avoid sleeping in a draft. Unless he's tied down, he just won't sleep in a draft, no matter what luxury accommodations have been prepared for him. His bed, if he has one of his own, should be placed off the floor in some semi-secluded spot. He loves privacy as much as he hates drafts.

He loves to drink, too, and fresh water should always be available to him. That's not an earth-shaking observation, but it's worthy of inclusion here for this curious reason: many rational people do not supply their cats with water. They supply it to dogs, chickens, canaries, horses, cows, goats, rabbits and any other forms of animal or vegetable life in their care, but not to cats.

Many cat owners claim that Felis catus is the most intelligent of all our domestic pets. Dog owners object on the grounds that the average dog is far easier to train than the average cat, but they forget that the dog is a natural joiner, whereas the cat is a natural loner. By nature, the dog is dependent and the cat independent. Hence the dog is more subservient and more willing to be trained.

A reasonable example of comparative degrees of intelligence would be a dog and a cat owned by John Doe. Let us assume that he trains both the dog and the cat to stay off a particular chair. I grant that it will take John Doe less time to train the dog to stay off the chair, but if he has patience he can also train the cat to do the same. So finally both dog and cat are trained to stay off the chair. When John Doe leaves the house, the dog will stay on the floor and the cat will jump on the chair. When John Doe returns and opens the door, both the dog and the cat will be on the floor.

Is the cat more intelligent than the dog? Of course. Is the cat more intelligent than John Doe? Sometimes I think so.

I am told that an average dog can be trained to do anything. I am willing to believe it, but not to accept it as proof of high intelligence. A cat can be trained to do anything that makes sense to him, and that's the reason he doesn't jump through a hoop of fire or jump on a horse's back for the amusement of human spectators (unless driven to do so by fear, as in the case of circus lions and tigers). The cat was around long before man, and if the need arises, he can do very well without man again. His brain, by the way, more closely resembles man's (in miniature) than does the dog's.

As pets go, the cat requires minimum care, little expense, and a great deal of affection. In return, he bestows joy, companionship and affection.

Welcome to the cat fancy.

Felis Catus Kind of Love

Chapter Eight

The cat's attitude toward romance is just as liberal and enthusiastic as the rabbit's.

The battle of the sexes begins at an early age for the female cat, or queen. On the average, she achieves puberty as early as six months (and before ten months). She can be ready much earlier. Cases of estrus at five months are not unusual.

In any event, when her first estrus (heat, or season) arrives, she's ready for mating. The period can last from three days to three weeks, and during it she is most anxious to become intimate with a gentleman. If she's owned by a cat fancier, she doesn't get the opportunity. One year is soon enough to breed a female, and professional breeders usually wait until the queen is at least two years old. Even after that, the serious breeders limit the queen's production to one litter a year as a safeguard for her health and longevity.

When estrus does occur, the queen's voice announces the glad tidings to the listening world. She "calls" in a peculiar series of cries that sound like laments to human ears and open invitations to the ears of any male cat within hearing. Her callings travel great distances and their range is beyond human hearing. Any tomcat hearing them forgets all other important business and sets his radar on the source.

City or country or suburb, wherever the queen lives, be sure that her calls will be answered. America is full of stray toms and pet toms who roam at will. If the queen in season is not confined, the toms will

surely arrive, and the nights in particular will be full of their pre-
liminary battle cries as they argue for the privilege of being first to
serve her. They always fight violently. None are cowards when a willing queen is the prize, and even a sadly beaten tom, if he still has
the strength, will engage his conqueror in combat when they meet
again at the next queen's door.

Rumors of two toms fighting to the death are heard now and again,
but no one ever provides the proof. I have witnessed many tomcats
in combat, and have seen them fight to the point of exhaustion, but
never death. They fight in silent fashion, and the caterwaulings and
cries one hears in the night are probably contributed by the specta-
tor toms and the appreciative queen. She knows they are fighting for
her favor and she approves. Be sure that the final, loudest cry of all
comes from her; it is her announcement that she and one tom have
consummated their love. She may make the same announcement a
few more times before the night is over.

The toms who answer her callings will probably be older than
the young queen. The average male is not ready to reproduce until
about one year, although a few reach puberty earlier (six months)
and tardy ones wait longer (eighteen months). He is at his prime as a
stud force between the ages of three and fourteen. The queen has
seven prime years for breeding: her second through eighth year,
although twenty-five-year old queens are on record as successful
mothers.

The culmination of the swift romance between queen and tom is
seldom an instant sort of thing. While a rough and ready, experienced tomcat may not appreciate them, the queen knows she's a
prize worth waiting for and she indulges in flirtatious, delaying tac-
tics: rolling, twisting, posing, strutting, rubbing.

If a picture is worth a thousand words, here are a few thousand
words from my camera:

Once feminine whims are satisfied, the actual mating occurs. Human assistance is neither necessary nor recommended, as it is in the case of a planned breeding, although standby supervision isn't a bad idea. The queen, exercising her traditional prerogative, may decide that the tomcat is not her dish of tea after all. If she turns on him, the tom will certainly object to her sudden change of mind and press his intentions. That's when the promise of cat love turns into a cat fight, and the combatants should be separated.

Fortunately, that rapid change of mood doesn't happen very often, and the queen sets the tableau for the mating by crouching before the tom. Her "calls" become beseeching moans and her back curves into a reverse arch or sway that leaves the head high and the rear higher than the head. She treads with her paws and flags her tail as the tom grips the back of her neck with his teeth, leaps astride her back and voices a small, contented cry of his own. His pelvic thrusts completed, he rests for a few moments while sperm ejaculation occurs, then withdraws his penis and slides from the queen's back. His retirement is always accompanied by a loud cry of pain from the queen, for the tom's penis is covered with recurved papillae that, on withdrawal, hurt and irritate the queen's vagina. Why nature planned this irritation is anybody's guess, and the educated guess of the experts is that it somehow stimulates ovulation.

126

Some students of cat nature claim that the lady's cries are misunderstood, and that she is simply giving voice to wild ecstasy. They point to the fact that great pain would discourage her ambition for more romance, and the truth is that most queens are ready for new courtship within hours—sometimes even minutes. Since cats have long memories, it may be that the queen overdoes things a bit with her cries and rollings and frantic activity. She may even turn on the tom, although a wise, experienced tom usually retreats to a safe perch in a hurry, or she may completely disregard him as she thrashes and jumps about before pausing to lick herself clean, relax, and look around for more action.

All that occurs, of course, when the breeding is supervised. As every country boy knows, there are times when the queen's calls attract a number of toms and long before she is disposed for mating, they will have decided (through fighting or threats) an order of precedence. If the queen does not retreat to a safe place after engaging the first tom, the next tom in line will grant her no time for relaxation. Most queens (if permitted) will mate several times a day for two or three days.

For the queen at liberty, then, the more toms the merrier, and its possible that each of the kittens in the litter will have a different father. She'll show no favoritism and take wonderful care of them all.

It doesn't happen too often, but the estrus period can occur again during her pregnancy—and if she's free to mate again, she certainly will. Thus it's possible for her to be double-pregnant, and astonishing results are on record: (1) the birth of two normal kittens followed by the birth of two normal kittens thirteen days later, and (2) the birth of four normal kittens and one embryo (three weeks old) at the same time.

If the tomcat worries about the queen's roving eye, he shouldn't. He is anything but a monogamist himself, and will mate more often than a queen in a given day if the opportunities arise. Professional catteries often carry one stud for thirty queens.

Once into puberty, the female cat's estrus periods occur in irregular fashion. Each queen has her own calendar, influenced somewhat by geographic location (length of days), and will normally have a minimum of two estrus periods a year, if bred each time. Some are almost continually in heat if not bred. There's just no telling, and despite expert thinking on an international scale, the number of periods for a particular female will always be a matter of speculation. If that seems mad, consider the derivation of the word *estrus:* it comes from the Greek word *oistros* and denotes anything that induces intense desire or madness.

The estrus or breeding season is defined as that period of the year in which females exhibit sexual activity, and studies have shown that it runs January–June in England, December–August in Algiers, and January–July in Northern United States.

Inspired by those studies, I kept complete records (1953–1964) on the breeding season of six of my own pet females: Mittens, Topsy, Beeline, Phyllis, Simba and Jigger. No attempt was made to control the matings, so natural conditions prevailed, and 72 live litters resulted.

Dates of estrus were calculated from the birth dates of those litters, and the records showed that 82 percent fell in the January–June period, and 87.5 percent in the month longer December–June span. November was the only month without a single estrus. The study proved, then, that December–June is the breeding season in Northern Virginia.

The normal gestation period is 62–63 days, although the range can be anywhere from 56 to 65 days, and to 70 days in exceptional cases. As a general rule, however, kittens born under 60 days are not likely to live.

The pregnant queen shows the first external signs of her condition about three weeks after coition: a slight enlargement and reddening of the nipples. The expert can gently probe the abdominal wall with his fingers along about then and feel the small, firm lumps, each a developing fetus. They'll be bigger but less firm after the fifth week, when the queen's abdomen begins to swell in proportions evident to even the unpracticed eye. Ten days later, it doesn't take an expert's probing fingers to verify the presence of the unborn kittens.

By that time, the appetite of the mother-to-be will have increased and an extra meal per day is required. All of her meals (usually three) should include extra calcium (milk, powdered bone meal, vitamin-mineral supplement), and the diet program should be observed right through the weaning of the kittens.

128

There's no need to carry her up a flight of stairs or to worry at all about her hurting herself through too much exercise. She'll pace herself and probably be just as lively as ever, but wary of jumping from heights. Many queens choose this period to roll over and over on the ground or floor. Nobody knows why. The activity doesn't harm the unborn kittens and the rollers enjoy it. If the queen is a longhair, now is the time to cut the hair away from around her nipples, leaving them free and clear for the nursing kittens in her future.

On or about the fiftieth day, the pregnant queen will start roaming the premises in quest of a suitable nesting place. If accommodations to her liking are not provided, she may stake out a claim to a closet or an open drawer or a dark corner behind some furniture. It's a time of extreme anxiety for her, and high time for her owner to give her peace of mind by providing adequate nursery quarters.

A large box will do, one big enough and wide enough for her to stretch out and still have room to spare. It can be of cardboard and should have both a top and a bottom. An easy entrance should be cut in one side or end—low enough for the queen's comings and goings, and high enough to keep her future crawling babies inside. The bottom should be lined with old newspapers, and then the box should be placed in a dark, quiet place. The cat wants darkness so that her young, when their eyes finally open, will not be damaged by too bright a light. Her want is instinctive, an instinct that is millions of years old.

More layers of newspaper will have to be added from time to time, for she will claw at the papers and shred them as she prepares the nest to her own satisfaction. She will busy herself with the nest all during the last few days before parturition, purring and talking to herself almost constantly, and also finding the time to demonstrate her affection for her owner, as if desirous of human reassurance that all is well. It is the one time when she is a little less independent. Sure, but not really sure, and grateful for attention from those she loves.

Sometimes that gratefulness is carried to the extreme, as in the case of my Foxy, who has always considered my bed the only proper place to have her kittens—and usually on top of me. Her nestbox was always ready, but at the last minute she preferred my company.

129

The arrival day of the kittens is heralded in advance. The cat's stomach drops perceptibly a full day before, and just hours before the kittening, a slight vaginal discharge occurs.

Finally, she retires to her nest and stays there. She fusses a bit, may even lap a bit of water or milk from a handy dish that should be in one corner, and talks to herself. She knows precisely what she's doing and what's expected of her, and probably won't need human assistance. Parturition is just another one of her natural functions.

Labor begins. It is not continuous, and the first contractions may not be noticed by a casual observer. Then the contractions become more frequent and stronger, and finally they evolve into a rhythm.

The queen pants as her labors detach the placentas containing the kittens from the walls of the cornu and push them through her central uterine tube and on to the vulva.

She strains and the first kitten is born.

There's no telling how long it will be before the last kitten is born.

The New Generation

Chapter Nine

The kitten arrives head first and wrapped in a paper thin, transparent, resilient sac. His mother, the queen, tears open the sack with her teeth, cuts the umbilical cord, then licks and rolls him vigorously until he starts breathing. Once satisfied that her newborn is alive, the queen does something that her ancestors have done for millions of years, and man isn't really sure why: she eats the afterbirth (placenta).

It's not an action peculiar to the cat, for dogs and other animals do the very same thing, and man has reasoned it out thus: (1) in the wild state, the mother would be unable to obtain food elsewhere for a considerable time; (2) in the wild state, the scent of the afterbirth might attract enemies; and, (3) the afterbirth may provide hormones needed for body functions or immunities.

By the time the queen has cleaned up the afterbirth, her firstborn has found one of her mammae and is already nursing. The kitten is blind and helpless, but not too helpless to find his first meal. As his mother relaxes to await the next birthing, he continues at his task. It's the only thing he does, when awake, for the next twenty-four hours.

In thirty minutes, or in an hour or several hours, the second kitten arrives head first and the queen repeats her actions. It's possible that

131

nature has dictated the maximum number of her new family: normally, the queen has eight mammae, and normally she'll have no more than eight kittens, and usually less. Two to four is average. My Jigger averaged 3.9 for a grand total of fifty-five kittens.

Sooner (a few hours) or later (a full day), the entire litter is born and busily nursing and sleeping. The queen won't stray from her box for another day, but she'll be hungry and she'll appreciate room service. She may even want a bite or a drink of milk in between giving birth to her kittens. Cats are independent and unpredictable even during kittening.

What I have described is a normal course of events during which the queen appreciates human company but requires no human help. It usually goes that way; but not always, and that's reason enough for somebody to be standing by when the queen's time arrives.

If it's her first experience, she may not rip the amniotic sac and cut the umbilical cord, and someone will have to do those things for her. If you're the one standing by, be gentle as you tear away the sac, and have sterilized, blunt scissors handy to cut the cord an inch or so from the kitten's body. Pinch the cord's end to stop the bleeding, then rub the kitten dry with a towel. If the kitten isn't breathing by then, hold him upside down to drain the mucus from his throat and keep rubbing. Once the kitten breaths, turn him over to his mother. The whole operation is simple. One doesn't need a medical degree.

The kitten may start arriving wrong end first. When that happens, it's usually with the first kitten to be born. This is a breech birth and against nature's law. The straining queen usually will be able to deliver the kitten only part way, but very gentle pulling, never force, should bring the kitten all the way. If this fails, call the veterinarian.

And call him, too, if the queen is in severe labor for over two hours without results. Saving the kittens may call for Caesarian section. Or call him if the queen's vaginal discharge (after the birth of her kittens) is dark and its odor foul—sure signs of infection; or if there have been more kittens than afterbirths, for any placenta that doesn't arrive can infect the queen.

Slim as it may seem, there's always the chance that the mother cat may not survive the kittening. Then the orphaned kittens will need immediate help in terms of food, warmth and care, and there's no time for procrastination.

If another lactating queen is handy, she may or may not accept the orphaned ones as her own, but it's always worth the try. Rubbing a bit of the foster mother's milk on the orphans' heads before they are introduced will help acceptance. And strange as it may seem, I have known brood bitches to accept kittens and raise them along with their pups. In composition, canine milk is reasonably close to cat milk.

But nine times out of ten, a foster mother will not be available, and the lives of the new orphans will be in the hands of humans. Milk must be supplied and served at close to body temperature (101.5°F). Fresh cow milk will do, but a better choice is evaporated milk (diluted 50–50), because of its high protein content. Evaporated goat milk is found at most pharmacies these days, and a friend of mine used it recently to bring through three Persians from the age of one hour.

If the orphans are to be bottle fed, then the size of the nipple should be no larger than the mother's nipple, usually a doll's nipple is proper size. An eye dropper can be used, but it means feeding a drop at a time to prevent fluid from entering the lungs. If neither method succeeds, then a twisted end of a handkerchief will. Soaked in milk first, of course.

For the first ten days or so, a little post-feeding care is required: gentle strokes (with a soft cloth or sponge) along the abdomen, front to rear. This is precisely what the mother cat does with her lickings, and in her absence somebody else must, for the slight pressures help the kittens with their excretions. And since there's no mother around to keep the nest box clean, somebody will have to change the soiled litter.

Until they are one week old, the orphan kittens must be fed every two hours 'round the clock. Each kitten will require about two cubic centimeters (half a teaspoon) of milk at every feeding. Both the quantity and the interval between feedings is increased during the second week, and by that time the responsible owner will have consulted the veterinanian for specific instructions.

But if all has gone well at the kittening, you might as well go to bed. Except for feeding the queen, there'll be nothing much to do for a few days. Don't handle the kittens, and don't try to clean the nest, the queen will handle everything. Just make sure that her husband or any other male cat keeps his distance. The gentlest of males will sometimes kill young kittens, and any queen worth her salt will attack any male within view. It's not the best of times for four footed men to be around the house, dogs included.

Day and night, the kittens feed at least a dozen times every twenty-four hours during their first days of life. Since they don't always feed at the same time, the mother has few free time-spans. It doesn't bother her. She'll sleep while all her kittens go right on nursing, and one or two of them may fall asleep with their mouths still full of nipple.

She's careful when she moves about, and never steps or treads or rolls on one of her young. That's quite a feat after the tenth day, when all the little eyes are open and the kittens start swimming around on their bellies.

Along about then, the mother cat doesn't mind human help in keeping the nest box clean. Old towels (replaced daily) over the litter is the usual solution.

Otherwise, the only help required by mother in the first four weeks is the preparation and serving of her daily meals. Although she'll care for the kittens all by herself for the next few weeks, after the thirtieth day its best for her if some relief is offered. So, during the fifth week, the kittens should be started on a meal of their own, a meal not supplied by mother. In every succeeding week, another daily meal is provided until, by the end of the eighth week, the kittens are on a four meals a day schedule and no longer dependent on mother. Now they are weaned.

The first weaning meal (at about thirty days) is sometimes the problem one. One kitten will make the switch from nipple to dish with ease, and another just won't understand. The latter must be helped, or taught, by rubbing a bit of the food on his nose or offering the food on a finger. Not hurrying the assistance sometimes makes it unnecessary, for the puzzled kitten will observe the dining one and follow his example.

The meals should always be served lukewarm and close to the cat's body temperature (101.5°F.) Here's a typical kitten weaning menu:

4th–5th weeks: cow or goat milk; add yolk of egg after 3rd day; serve once a day.

5th–6th weeks: add pablum to above; serve twice a day.

134

6th–7th weeks: baby meats, finely cut fresh kidney and pablum (50–50) with egg yolk and sufficient whole milk to create mush; serve three times a day.

7th–8th weeks: baby meats, finely cut meats and baby vegetables or soft-cooked cereals (50–50) with egg yolk and milk; serve four times a day.

Dietary sense comes to the kitten at an early age. He won't overeat (but may as an adult), but every kitten in a litter will not eat the same amount.

After he's weaned, his meals become larger and the number of meals is cut down. A pretty good rule of thumb: four meals a day until the fourth month, then three meals until the eighth month, and two meals a day from there to one year. From there on it's one or two meals a day, depending on the individual cat.

As he grows to adulthood, the kitten needs and consumes more food per day than he will as an adult, and all during his growing period his diet should contain at least 37 percent protein.

Growth is greatest during the first nine months, then it tapers off until the sixteenth month, when the average cat is as big as he's ever going to be. His milk teeth will have been replaced by the permanents along about the sixth month, and from then on his diet is the same as an adult's, except for more meals per day.

His adult personality is the sum total of his natural instincts and the environment of his kittenhood. We humans are responsible for that environment, and if he matures into a bum we have only ourselves to blame.

From the moment he enters one's life and home as a kitten, he must be recognized for what he is: an independent fellow who is not a dog or a child or a monkey, and is even quite unlike any kitten one may have owned before. He's different. He's a special case.

The new kitten in one's life cannot be rushed. It's important to establish friendship and to start teaching him where he can and cannot roam, but none of those things can be accomplished in an hour or a day. One just has to be patient.

I would advise treating the youngster almost as if he wasn't there. The only direct actions for the first few days should be the serving of his meals and attending to his housebreaking. The meals will establish friendship soon enough.

Many things are basic to the cat, and habit is one of them. Even the kitten wants his food served at the same time and in the same place every day. His comfort station, his water bowl, his bed, all should have permanent posts.

Curiosity is a strong basic, and it leads the new kitten into exploring every square inch of the premises. If he's not supposed to be someplace—on a table or chair, perhaps—he won't know it unless he's removed from it, time after time, and scolded by a soft (never angry) voice. He'll learn. Habit again.

That curiosity can be fatal if the master is careless. Too many kittens and cats fall out of windows to their death, and even more kittens and cats fall victims to poison made available (unintentionally) by their owners than to poison offered (intentionally) by cat haters.

Young Felis catus' inquisitiveness can get him into all sorts of trouble in the great outdoors, and even if he's living in the country, an enclosure is safest for him when his play isn't being supervised. Nobody has told him about bees and hornets. He doesn't know, nor do his elders, that it just isn't safe to cross a road, not when so many drivers will deliberately swerve out of their way to run over the traffic-wise cat or dog waiting patiently at the side of the road. Nor has the kitten read about the mighty hunters with rifles who consider any cat fair game, or the good citizens in the neighborhood who are ailurophobes at heart and set out poisoned foods, or the loose dogs wandering around with destruction on their minds, or the men who prowl about stealing pets for laboratories.

Always keep an eye on a kitten when he's outdoors. He's not looking for trouble, but trouble can find him.

Affection, both giving and receiving, is a vital kitten basic. The new kitten will come to one soon enough, and that's the time to pet him and play with him and establish firm friendship. Time, too, to warn the children in the family that the kitten is not made of stainless steel and that his tail is not a handle.

I'm a great believer in children or I wouldn't be a father, and I don't believe any family should put the kitten before the child. Still, the sad truth is that too many kittens are brought to their new homes as playthings or living toys for children.

It never works. The kitten is a baby, not a toy. It doesn't take much to frighten him, and he'll either run or react in a defensive manner. Continued maltreatment in his formative months will turn him into a nervous wreck or an unpredictable animal, and neither make the best of pets.

In millions of homes, children are taught that the kitten is another member of the family and should be treated as such. A child and a kitten, a child and a cat, they make fine companions if the relationship starts in the right way.

Most of the benefits accrue to the child. One who understands the kitten is sure to appreciate all animals. And I would guess that the child who grasps all the complexities of Felis catus may have a little less trouble solving the problems he's bound to face in life.

And what about at kitten for the childless home?

I recommend two.

There's no place like a home with kittens.

Caterwaulings and Cautions

Chapter Ten

Almost everyone has known an Uncle Ned, the man who was never ill in his lifetime, lived to a ripe old age and even then didn't die a natural death—he was hit on the head by a falling safe and never knew what hit him.

There are many Uncle Neds in the cat world. They lead healthy, happy lives, never knowing how fortunate they are. Their owners are fortunate, too, for cats that are *always* healthy belong to a minority group.

The penalty for thousands of years of domestication is *disease*. Cats are susceptible to (and carriers of) many serious diseases, and that is the best of all arguments for keeping the pet cat indoors as much as possible. He loves the outdoors, but indoors prevents him from association with other cats who may carry contagion, to say nothing of infected rodents and other animals and poisoned foods.

Every owner of a cat, including the lucky owners of Uncle Neds, should have some basic knowledge of the most serious diseases so that he may recognize them and take prompt action.

And that prompt action should always be an immediate visit (with the sick cat) to a veterinarian. Thanks to the great strides made by veterinary medicine in recent years, some of the diseases that were once fatal can now be cured, if not prevented.

Here are the important ones, the critical ones, the ones to watch for:

Panleukopenia. Commonly known as feline enteritis it has had a host of other names, but under any alias the disease is worldwide and so highly contagious that it can become a plague among cats in a given community, so strong and lasting that a healthy cat can pick up the virus left by an infected cat in a room during the previous year. Fortunately, about forty percent of all cats are immune to it, and vaccines exist to assure passive (temporary) or active immunity. Unfortunately, there are no sure symptoms of the disease during its incubation period, and when it strikes, the adult cat has less than an even chance of survival and a kitten hardly any chance. The disease amounts to a rapid decrease in the white blood cell count and results in high fever (104° or above), loss of appetite, vomiting and general weakness. Immediate treatment by a veterinarian is vital, but prevention is a wiser course and only a foolish owner will bring home an unvaccinated kitten.

Rabies. Acute and contagious, it is common to most mammals, birds and man. While much more prevalent in dogs, some cases are reported every year. In most cases, the disease is transmitted by bites from other rabid animals, and cats can infect man through bites. Rabies is a brain inflammation known as encephalitis, and its symptoms are associated with madness: biting, hiding, frenzy, convulsions and final paralysis. There's no cure, but there is a preventative vaccine. Some states require the vaccination of all animals imported from other states, and most states require the reporting (to the local public health authority) of humans bitten by rabid animals.

Pseudorabies. Another dangerous, infectious disease that is not confined to cats and has its highest incidence rate among rats. Thus, cats who eat rats are destroying the main source of the disease and running the risk of catching it, too. Except for absence of viciousness, the symptoms are similar to those of rabies. Since most authorities agree that infection must be through ingestion, control of the cat's diet is the logical preventative, and so is destroying the local rat population.

Rhinotracheitis. Better known as FVR (Feline Viral Rhinotracheitis), it's highly contagious, relatively new (1958) to the United States,

144

and the cat is its only known host. It spreads from the sneezes of infected cats. Sneezing, nasal discharge, loss of weight, conjunctivitis and lachrymation are its signs. Cats under eighteen months of age are its favorite targets. So far, there's no vaccine for FVR. Morbidity varies from almost 100 percent in kittens to a very low rate in old cats.

Pneumonitis. It's so close to other viral respiratory infections that clinical diagnosis is sometimes impossible. While highly contagious, the mortality rate is low and kittens are the chief victims. High fever, eye and nasal discharge, coughing and sneezing are its symptoms. An immunity vaccine is available and should be followed by annual booster shots.

These are the major viral diseases any cat should be happy to avoid. There are others, but none as dangerous or as widespread. Viral disease weakens the resistance of the cat and a second set of diseases, bacterial ones, may enter the picture as secondary infections. There is a small army of these bacterial diseases, and two are reason enough for owners to stay on the alert:

Tuberculosis. Cats are more susceptible to bovine-type than to human-type tuberculosis, the incidence ratio in the United States being about twenty to one. Infected milk fed to the cat is the chief source of the bovine-type, but thanks to the pasteurization of milk almost everywhere in this country, the type occurs infrequently and runs to about 150 cases per year. Sneezing, fever, anemia and loss of weight are all symptoms, and a cat so afflicted should be examined by a veterinarian. If the diagnosis points to this disease, it's best to have the cat put to sleep. The disease is highly contagious and can be transmitted to other animals and to man. The Siamese seems to be more susceptible to both types than are the other breeds.

Trench Mouth. A highly contagious disease that occurs quite frequently. Symptoms include tartar on the teeth, bleeding gums, ulcerations and often loss of teeth. Young adult Siamese are particularly susceptible and bear watching. The usual treatment consists of dental care and the administration of penicillin. Disinfection and cleansing of the feeding bowls of afflicted cats will help prevent the spread of the disease. Isolation from other cats and animals until the disease is conquered is a must.

And then there are the fungal diseases which most of us think of as skin infections. Cat lovers hate to admit it, but cats are responsible for about ninety percent of the skin infections that make life miserable for cats, other animals, and man.

The one to watch for is *Ringworm* (a misnomer, since no worm is involved), commonest of the skin infections shared by cat and man. If remedial steps are not taken, the infection spreads over the entire body, starting with the head and forequarters. The four infection types all have the same symptoms: loss of hair in small patches, scaliness, scabs, and a great deal of scratching by the cat. The owner who notices ringworm on his own hand should be able to put two and two together.

Other skin infections occur infrequently in cats, but the same cannot be said for *Parasites,* those low forms of life that live within or upon higher forms of life. Over five hundred different types, internal and external, find the cat—and dog—attractive hosts. Most are unimportant to him, but a few can run riot and kill.

Felis catus is the involuntary host to a large variety of internal parasites known as worms. All of them spell trouble, and a few are dangerous: *Roundworms* are commonest, and one species (trichinella spiralis) causes trichinosis in both cats and man. The worm can come from raw pork and raw pork kidneys, so only cooked pork and pork parts are safe for the cat. These worms multiply at an alarming rate. *Hookworms* are the blood and tissue eaters and can kill a kitten and weaken an adult to the point of death. The dangerous *Tapeworms* require intermediate hosts and are best controlled by controlling the cat's fleas and lice.

If a day in court were given to all the kinds of worms that infest cats all the worms would be found guilty of working against the best interests of their hosts. The whole subject of worms is an unpleasant one to most people, but like the mountain, it is there, and it is important to every cat and every cat owner. Fortunately, the problem—and it should be regarded as a problem—can be solved by your favorite veterinarian, who has the answers and the medicines to take care of every type of worm, and the means to determine which types are currently present. Cats are much more sensitive than dogs to the toxic effect of medicines, and professional advice is always the safest course. Whether you are a new owner or a veteran owner, don't assume your cat is wormless.

And that brings us to the external parasites—the fleas and lice and mites and ticks that even the non-experts can see:

Fleas. Four species infest cats: the cat flea, the dog flea, the human flea, and the sticktight flea. Each prefers its own host, but it doesn't discriminate and when the preferred host is absent it will look around for another. Only the sticktight flea stays put, preferring the less hairy regions about the ears and the eyes. The other three are roamers and are found all over the cat's body. The cat who is continually scratching, licking and biting himself has too many fleas and may be developing severe flea dermatitis.

Since fleas drown in a few minutes, bathing the cat is a convenient way to deflea him. Some insecticides and powders are also effective, but the user should be wary: DDT, lindane and chlordane are among popular ingredients that can poison the cat, for he's sure to lick his coat. But defleaing is valueless unless all fleas and flea eggs are removed from the cat's sleeping and living quarters. A vacuum cleaner is helpful for that purpose.

During the warm months, the battle against fleas on the cat who goes outdoors must be continuous. That rule applies for all average cats. There are very special cats, not many, whose personalities do not appeal to fleas. You'll never find a flea on such a cat. A fortune awaits the person who can solve the riddle.

Mites are external parasites, too, and they are more specialized in their work than fleas. There are several types, and each type has its specialty. The cat who shakes his head in a frenzied manner and constantly scratches his ears is suffering from an infestation of *otodectes cynotis,* or ear mites. These potentially dangerous tiny villains work through the ear canal and bore into the tender skin near the eardrum. Bloody crusts, caused by the scratching, may form on or near the ears, and the ear interiors contain a brown, foul, waxy matter. Treated in time, the condition clears rapidly.

The specialty of the skin-burrowing mite known as *notoedres cati* is the production of mange—known as scabies in man and easily transferred from cat to man. The females lay their eggs under the skin and the larvae hatch and feed there, and then the cycle begins all

147

over again. The cat's head is the prime target area of these mites, and if he scratches and rubs his head continually it's high time to investigate.

The oddest of the mites, and the most difficult to detect, is *cheyetiella parasitivorax*. It functions as a parasite of the mange mites, a parasite's parasite, so to speak. The cats are not concerned with it and usually show no sign of infection. Strangely, its presence is announced by a rash on the hands of the human who handles the cat.

Lice are right behind mites in order of importance. *Felicola subrostratus* is the name, or cat louse. It's so small that it may go unnoticed. It bites and it irritates the adult cat, but its presence becomes dangerous where kittens are concerned. An infested mother cat will serve as a launching pad for the louse, and when they land on the kittens they go to work—often with fatal results. Dustings with rotenone powder is an effective treatment, and the dustings should continue for several days. The eggs, as well as the lice must be destroyed. This is a very persistent parasite.

The *tick* is another story. It's big enough to be seen, or to be felt when one is petting a cat. The longer it stays on the cat, the bigger it gets (as it swells on the host's blood). While infestations in the cat are infrequent, it takes only one tick to pass along a number of common diseases, including the dangerous Rocky Mountain spotted fever. It should be removed carefully so that the head is not left under the skin as a potential source of infection. Pinch the tick with a piece of cotton (saturated with rubbing alcohol) until it releases itself, then kill it. Most of us are apt to regard ticks as residents of the countryside, but they are fairly well distributed all over the United States these days. The fact is that they are both rural and urban, and a cat or dog can pick one up on the streets of Manhattan.

There are two other external parasites common enough for inclusion here: the *botfly* and the *blowfly*. The larva of each grows under the skin causing an infection that often feels, to the touch, like a hard lump.

If this chapter leads the reader to the conclusion that a cat's state of health is dependent upon his owner's constant observation, the conclusion is correct. And if my recommendations of the veterinarian seem frequent, it is because only he has the knowledge and facilities and medicines to deal safely with the specific maladies. On the other hand, many of the things that happen to a cat can be safely treated at home. The average home medicine cabinet has the tools, so to speak, to remedy a cut or constipation or a splinter. Stay calm, keep the cat calm, and use the same common sense that you would use in treating a baby.

Still, never forget the veterinarian, especially if you know your cat is not an Uncle Ned and you suspect:

Tumors. Cats are subject to many different types of tumor, some benign, some malignant, and all spreading and growing in a clinical course similar to tumors in man. There's no ready answer, but the incidence rate is higher in the United States than elsewhere in the world. Tumors in cats are more prevalent than believed even a few years ago. Unfortunately, malignant types are more common than the benign. Growths or lumps on the skin—anywhere on the cat's body—are the trouble signs and require prompt examination.

Anemia. Of all domestic animals, cats suffer the most from anemia. And of those cats who do suffer, about fifty percent have feline infectious anemia. Fleas are the usual agents, carrying the infection from a sick cat to a healthy cat. Symptoms include fever, rapid loss of weight, weakness and depression.

Hip Dysplasia. This deformity of the hip has a long history in other larger animals and in man, but has been encountered in cats only in recent years and mostly in the Siamese. If current knowledge of other animals holds true with cats, the condition is usually detected before six months. With the exception of mild cases, improper movement (weak, awkward) of the quarters will be noticeable. Heredity is believed to be the cause in most cases, and the breeding of an affected animal should be avoided. There is no known cure, and there isn't likely to be one, although muscles may compensate in cases that are not extreme. So far as cats are concerned, the control of the affliction would appear to be in the hands of responsible breeders and their willingness to radiograph all breeding stock.

Eczema. Dermatitis is its other name, an inflammation of the skin that comes wet and dry and can spread like wildfire. Its source can be almost anything: a scratch, a flea bite, bacterial infection, nutritional deficiency or allergy, or a chemical picked up on the lawn.

149

The skin is scaly and crusty, and watery in the case of the wet form. It's itchy, and the cat responds with scratching, and that serves to spread it even more. It will not cure itself and go away. Professional help is needed; then it can be cured.

Cystitis. Inflammation of the bladder, a common problem in the cat world, is more serious with the male than the female. The original infection is often joined by stones forming in the urethral passages and causing a blockage. Nobody knows where these stones come from, but they are composed of minerals and they must be removed, either by surgery or dissolving. The cat will urinate frequently, or at least try to, and show definite signs of discomfort and pain. The owner who suspects cystitis shouldn't wait around until he's absolutely sure. The cat may be dead by that time.

The cats pictured here do not have cystitis. They are very healthy cats. They don't have anything.

Well, a flea or two perhaps. Nothing more.

Brad-Mar's Naeng Noi, Korat, female.
Owner: Marie E. Purdy.

The Nonconformist Gourmand

Chapter Eleven

The surest way to keep a cat healthy, to turn him into an Uncle Ned even if he was born under an unlucky star, is to keep him in top condition. A strong body is the best defense against all the ailments, deadly or minor, that seem so intent on pursuing and torturing Felis catus.

Well conditioned cats are properly fed cats, of course, and they are supreme as pets. Their coats are smooth and glossy, their eyes are bright, they are playful and alert, they produce fine kittens and they live a long time. Just the opposite can be said of the poorly fed cats, the ones that never measure up to their owners' expectations as even moderately satisfactory pets.

So it behooves all cat owners to have at least some grasp of the cat's nutritional requirements—what to feed him and what not to feed him.

Our present day knowledge is based largely on cat history. All during the millions of years before he accepted man as his benefactor, the carnivorous Felis catus existed on a diet of small animals, birds, insects, fish, and lizards. He devoured all of their edible parts, and in the doing added the vegetable contents of their digestive tracts to his diet. His one additional source of vegetation, apparently, was grass.

151

It's difficult to argue with such success, and man hasn't improved too much on that original diet. We still feed meat and fish and fowl and the innards, plus such vegetables as the cat will accept. For some strange reason, scientific studies of the nutritional requirements of the cat have lagged far behind all the other domesticated animals, plus the rat and the mouse. Things are looking up, however, and several depth studies have been launched in recent years. We know a great deal more about the cat's nutritional needs than we did ten years ago, and the progress is continuing.

This is fortunate, for left to his own devices, there's no telling what the individual cat will or will not eat. Somewhere along the way, Felis catus has lost his natural instinct for the foods that are good and bad for him, and "Wise as a cat" does not apply to his table. His owner must supply all the wisdom through selection and offering of the foods containing the proper nutrients. It's not difficult.

Of the six classes of nutrients, the cat requires five: proteins, fats, vitamins, minerals and water. Number six, carbohydrates (starches and sugars) are difficult for him to digest and are apparently not essential to him although they can provide energy. He'll eat them though, and I sometimes feed a little potato or vegetable to my cats and have noted neither harm nor benefit.

152

A high protein content in his diet is a must (30 to 40 percent for adults), for this nutrient sustains the greatest number of body functions. Lean meats, *cooked* fish and poultry, milk, cheese and eggs are all fine protein foods.

Most recent studies favor a high fat content (25 to 30 percent) as found in fatty meats, oils, butter and margarine. Fats make food more palatable, provide energy and muscle strength, and provide vitamin A, an absolute necessity for growth, vision, skin, teeth, and resistance to infection. Liver, cream and egg yolk are also rich sources of vitamin A.

His other nutritional (vitamin) requirements include:

Vitamin B_1 (thiamine), found in most fish and all meats, and particularly in lean pork and beef liver. Overcooking can destroy it (15 minutes for lean pork is sufficient).

Vitamin B_2 (riboflavin), found in meats, vegetables, grains and milk. Without it, the cat becomes highly nervous and wastes away.

Vitamin B_6, found in the other B sources, and necessary for the breakdown of proteins.

Niacin, essential to survival and supplied by meats, poultry, fish, flour and cereals.

Panthothenic acid which utilizes the other nutrients, and choline, essential for utilization of the fats. Liver, kidney, heart, and eggs are the best sources for both.

Vitamin D, the cat's insurance against rickets and malformation of teeth and bones, comes from fish liver oils, marine fish, liver, butter and eggs.

Vitamin E, a basic vitamin for growth and survival, and found in wheat germ oils, cereals, egg yolk and beef liver. Continued E deficiency leads to steatitis, a painful and usually fatal disease.

Vitamin C (ascorbic acid) is not required by cats, and the cats must know it. Most of them turn up their noses at citrus.

Felis catus is no different from any other animal, he needs his minerals. Six percent of his body is composed of calcium, phosphorus, potassium, sodium, chlorine, magnesium and sulfur. He requires other minerals in lesser amounts, and each serves a specific purpose. Since they are not stored (the daily excess is secreted), a constant supply is needed. Fortunately, a planned diet lacking sufficient minerals would be difficult to achieve.

Water, the fifth essential nutrient, is the most underrated of all. It constitutes seventy percent of his body weight and all of his body functions require it. Next to oxygen, water is the cat's most important requirement for survival, and a supply of fresh water should always be available for him. Milk is not an adequate substitute. The cat can survive without food for weeks, but he can't last for many days without water.

The rule of thumb for an adult cat's feeding schedule is one or two meals a day, and the rule for quantity is common sense and observation—the cat should be neither fat nor too lean, and most remain at their proper weight on not more than seven ounces of food a day.

Actually, two meals a day are unnecessary. I know this as well as the next fellow and go right on feeding nine of my eleven cats two meals a day. The others, both males, prefer a single meal; one insists on dining in the morning, the other in the evening.

The one exception to the adult feeding schedule is the pregnant queen. She always needs two meals, and after six weeks she may require three. She definitely needs three after the kittens are born and until they are weaned, and even so, she'll lose some weight.

If the foods mentioned are the basic ones to feed the cat, and they are, then the one problem to be resolved concerns the manner of serving them: cooked or uncooked? This question has provided the cat fancy with a never ending debate, and exponents for each side back their claims with examples of healthy, happy cats.

Those who feed raw foods consider that they are following nature's laws, for certainly the cat's first diet was raw. They point, too, to the "cooked away" nutritional losses of cooked foods, and that is certainly a valid point. Still, the cooked food theorists insist that more than an adequate amount of nourishment remains.

Today, thanks to a recent, exhaustive study of several generations of cats, the raw food school of thought would appear to be the right one. The study proved that uncooked foods produced better growth, development, reproduction and lactation. Raw meat and milk proved superior to cooked meat and milk. As far as those two foods go, the superior diet parallels the one my cats have been thriving on for years. Here's what I feed my cats and can recommend for yours:

Meats:	Raw beef, veal, lamb and horsemeat, fat included. Cut into small pieces. *Cooked* pork, on occasion. Also raw beef kidney, liver and heart. I feed my cats an average of six ounces of raw fresh beef kidney per day.
Fish:	Always cooked, with a preference for the saltwater varieties. Small pieces, and always boned.
Poultry:	Raw or cooked chicken, turkey, duck, squab. Small pieces and little bones removed. Usually it is cooked and amounts to the leftovers. Don't feed the skins.
Milk:	By itself or mixed right in with the other food for those of my cats who will accept it. Never serve ice cold. Some adult cats avoid milk as if it were poison. Evaporated milk acts as a cathartic for some cats, but reconstituted powdered milk does not.
Vegetables:	All vegetables, cooked or raw can be offered. Potatoes should be *cooked* and mashed. Oat sprouts grown indoors are liked by most cats, and a touch of catnip every week serves as a treat. Remember that the cat is not a vegetarian, and that cat tastes vary, and some are anti-vegetable. Carrots are ice cream to one cat and bricks to another.
Eggs:	Hard or soft boiled or raw eggs whipped in milk. I offer cottage cheese as a treat now and then, not as a part of the regular diet.

No matter what diet formula one uses for his cats, other cat lovers are bound to ask, "Are you sure that your cats are getting enough vitamins and minerals?" One can be sure and still not be absolutely sure, and rather than stay awake nights wondering, many owners fortify the cat's daily food ration with vitamin-mineral supplements. The supplements come in liquid, tablet or powder form, and anyone using them should forget the adage, "If a little is good, a lot is better." An amount that proves sufficient (or harmless) for one cat may prove to be an excess dosage for another. There's no danger in extra minerals or B vitamins, since the cat doesn't store what he doesn't need, but an excess of some vitamins (A, D and E) has been

155

known to produce unhappy results. Proceed with caution, that's the best advice for anyone using, or planning to use, the supplements.

The major producers of cat foods are familiar with the diet requirements, and much of the continuing research is being conducted in their laboratories. The fact remains, however, that some of the many commercial foods are not balanced, and the safest course for those in doubt is to place faith in several, so that no one single brand dominates the diet, and then to supplement those brands with fresh foods.

There will always be independent thinking cats who will refuse the most appetizing commercial or home prepared meals. They will sniff and refuse to taste and turn away in a disdainful manner, unimpressed by man's new knowledge of the feline population's nutritional requirements. But even the stubbornest of cats can be trained to eat what's proper for them, although it takes patience and sometimes causes needless worry.

Thus, if a cat refuses to eat (and an adult often does just that in strange surroundings), the food should be removed after a few minutes, kept fresh, and then offered again the next day. The process is repeated until the cat finally eats. And he will. He may be stubborn but he's not a fool.

The Id, as in Felid

Chapter Twelve

One could spend a lifetime searching the world, in vain, for a pair of carbon copy cats. Among the several hundred million cats who share this earth with us, there are some who appear to be exact replicas—in color and weight and tail and coat and general conformation—but no two cats will ever be precisely alike.

The difference lies in personality. It may be a matter of feline pride, but whatever the reason, the cat's personality starts developing very early in life and is firmly developed long before adulthood.

Anyone who has observed the development of a given litter of kittens will agree that identical inheritance factors and identical environment somehow produce diverse personalities. It may not seem reasonable, but that's the way it is. It doesn't take long to recognize the bold ones and the shy ones and the ones in between. All may be playful, but each will be playful in his own degree, and sometimes the bully is the smallest one in the litter. A subtle social order develops, and it's most noticeable at feeding time, when the strong minded ones arrive at the meal first.

So no two cats are ever alike: the id of one is never the id of another. That is the unwritten law of Felis catus, and I suspect it also holds true for all his cousins in the cat family tree.

This is something to remember when the time comes to replace one's long-time pet, for the newcomer will not be the same as the

157

departed old-timer, and a comparison is unfair. The newcomer may look the same as to breed and color and eyes and all the rest, but be very sure that his personality is different and thus his tastes and reactions will be different. Any adjusting will most likely come from the owner.

To those who know that the time is not far-off for replacing the veteran, I would recommend bringing the new kitten home now. It amounts to insurance against the saddest of days, and the oldster may even condescend to teach the youngster a few things about your way of life and your odd reaction to finding a cat on the dining·room table. It will help you, too, in learning to accept the new and different personality.

Feline ids are closest in the area defined as the spirit of independence, but even here the spirit varies in each cat. The fancy's philosophers have long wondered why the cat remains so independent, since the need is no longer there, at least not for pet cats. As for myself, I have always thought that the cat has remained his own true self because he has never been quite sure of man. His eyes continue to tell me that. He enjoys the easy living and appreciates our efforts in his behalf, but he must regard us as strange and inferior beings. I don't think he accepts his pet status, for we seem to be his servants: feeding him, caring for him, opening doors for him, and seeing to his every comfort. He is ready, just as he is, for any kind of weather, but we lack fur and must don all sorts of idiotic garments. Dining is a simple matter to him, but what must he think of our elaborate preparations, our pots and pans and tools, our odd habit of always sitting at a table? And surely he is amused to see us stumbling about in a dark room.

He has his reasons to feel superior. And if the news has been handed down through all the generations, then he may be laughing at us. Man once considered him a deity, but he's never held man in such high esteem.

I think it's safe to assume that the cat has accepted man. Not every cat will agree, of course, and current dissenters will be found among the thousands of strays who do very well for themselves. If he respects us at all, and his times of affection signal that he does, it may be because he suspects that we are some sort of distant relation. Cat and

159

man do share an amazing number of similarities, and a mutual craving for comfort is just one of them. We both have a brain, a central nervous system, a four-chambered heart and circulatory system, the same internal organs, a nose, paired lungs, and a long list of the same bones—from cranium to ribs to vertebrae. And we are both mammals and both intelligent.

How intelligent is another story, but the similarity is still there, for there are smart humans and smart cats, and stupid humans and stupid cats, too.

I consider the average cat a very intelligent animal, and I'm willing to let it go at that. All sorts of experiments have been conducted to test the comparative intelligence of animals, and some have indicated that Felis catus rates second only to man. But of necessity, all such examinations are controlled and held under man-invented, unnatural conditions, and for all one knows some of the animals may have been oafs.

So I am content to remain apart from all controversy, and confess only to my wife that the cat is more intelligent than most other animals.

I would not admit the same to my cats.

Cat Lovers' Corner

Chapter Thirteen

If all that you have read and seen on the preceding pages has stimulated your interest or deepened your love and understanding of the domestic cat, I am content, and I think Shawnee Moonflight, who was kind enough to write a delightful introduction to my book, will be too. If I have played some role in making the relationship between man and felis catus a stronger one, my efforts have been rewarded.

This final chapter is no more than a library of information which has its proper place in a book that is to be useful to cat lovers, but would have delayed the proceedings if inserted elsewhere. Whether you're interested in a cat club in Albuquerque or in the Cat of the Year winner of 1947 (Wimauma Masterpiece of Chalsu), you will find it by turning to the Cat Lovers' Corner.

I'll start with my own partiality for "catography," and the interested reader can come along as I offer some tips along with some of my favorite shots.

Believe it or not, she's only yawning.
Hasselblad, 80mm. lens; Ektachrome film; exposure, f22; electronic flash lighting, 1/500 sec.

I took the kitten upstairs, but Foxy had other ideas.
Rolleiflex; Plus-X film; exposure, f22, 1/500 sec.; lighting, three "Speed Midget" flash bulbs, 1/200 sec.

To get this shot, I put a cat—who obviously does not enjoy the water—on a rock in the shallow section of a near-by creek.
Rolleiflex; Plus-X film.

Just before Topsy was about to yawn, I placed the kitten on her. When she yawned, I snapped.
Hasselblad, 80mm. lens; Plus-X film; exposure, f22, electronic flash lighting, 1/500 sec.

I was lucky enough to have the camera aimed in Jigger's direction, when she slipped off the branch of a tree. Jigger was lucky enough to only fall a short distance and land on her feet.

Rolleiflex, Plus-X film, distance, 11 feet; exposure, f5.6, 1/500 sec.

All they're after is their breakfast.
Rolleiflex Tri-X film; exposure, f11, distance, 12 to 15 feet; electronic flash, 1/500 sec.

A yawn, plus simulated nighttime.
Rolleiflex; Superhypan film; exposure, f16, 1/250; electronic flash, 1/500 sec.

The eyes are mine. At a show, my wife overheard a viewer say, "Those eyes look almost human."

Rolleiflex; Plus-X film; f22; 1/100 sec.; distance 5 feet; two "Speed Midget" flash bulbs.

These kittens were put into position while they were sleeping. The picture was taken as soon as they woke up. Hasselblad with 80mm. lens; 4 electronic flash lights; Plus-X film; exposure, f22, 1/500 sec.

Six black and white and three color transparencies were used to make this.
Hasselblad camera with Extension Bellows and Reproadapter, Electronic flash lighting; Ektachrome color film
and Plus-X black and white film. All transparencies mounted between glass, 2¼x2¼ inch.

The national cat organizations? They are the governing bodies that register purebred cats in this country, and they sanction and rule the cat shows sponsored by their respective member clubs. These are the seven that guide the cat fancy in the United States, and information about shows, breeds and breeders may be obtained from any or all of them:

AMERICAN CAT FANCIERS ASSOCIATION, INC.,
Central Office: 1104 Bouldin Avenue
        Austin, Texas 78704

AMERICAN CAT ASSOCIATION, INC.,
Recorder-Treasurer: Mrs. Stanley Gibson
        Lakeside, Berrien Co.,
        Michigan 49116

CAT FANCIERS ASSOCIATION, INC.,
Central Office: Riverhill Building,
        39 East Front St.,
        Red Bank,
        New Jersey 07701

CROWN CAT FANCIERS FEDERATION,
Secretary: Whitney D. Abt,
        Burton, Texas

CAT FANCIERS FEDERATION, INC.,
Secretary: R. P. Orman,
        P. O. Box 8763
        Philadelphia,
        Pennsylvania 19105

NATIONAL CAT FANCIERS ASSOCIATION, INC.,
Central Office: 8219 Rosemont,
        Detroit,
        Michigan 48228

UNITED CAT FEDERATION, INC.,
Secretary: Mrs. Sherman Arps,
        15716 Addison,
        Encino,
        California 91316

The national cat association of Canada is:
CANADIAN CAT ASSOCIATION
P. O. Box 553
Ottawa, Ontario

The member clubs are found in all parts of the country. Anyone with more than a casual interest in cats should belong to his local or nearest club. Membership can sometimes result in unexpected benefits, as in the case of the man who moved to a new community and encountered difficulties in (1) increasing his mortgage, (2) entering his son in a private school, (3) finding a trustworthy baby sitter, and (4) getting into the social swim. He joined the nearest cat club and found that his fellow members included a banker, a director of the school, a baby sitter and the local leader of society. All of his problems were solved. Herewith, some of the important all-breed cat clubs and the specialty cat clubs active in this country and Canada:

Alabama

Hallmark Cat Fanciers, Tuskegee (CCFF)

Heart of Dixie Cat Club, Montgomery (ACFA)

Arizona

Canyon State Cat Club, Phoenix (ACA)

Tucson Cat Club, Tucson, (ACA)

San Marcos Cat Club, Chandler (ACA)

Arizona Cat Club, Phoenix (ACFA)

California

Contra Costa Cat Fanciers, Richmond (ACA)

Cosmopolitan Cat Club, El Monte (ACA)

Pacific Cat Fanciers, Bell (ACA)

Pan Pacific Cat Club, Nowalk (ACA)

Sequoia Cat Fanciers, San Jose (ACA)

Sierra Cat Fanciers, Lafayette (ACA)

Spanish Trail Tabby-Torty, Whittier (ACA)

Cal Coast Cat Club, San Juan Capistrano (ACFA)

El Gato Cat Fanciers, Los Gatos (ACFA)

Silvergate Cat Club, San Diego (ACFA)

El Dorado Cat Club, Rosemead (ACFA)

Zuma Cat Club, Woodland Hills (ACFA)

North California Friendly Felines, Chico (ACFA)

Los Conquistadores Cat Club, Concord (ACFA)

City of Angels Cat Fanciers, Sunland (ACFA)

Land of Verdugos Cat Club, Los Angeles (CFF)

Pacific Cat Club, San Francisco (CFF)

St. Francis Cat Fanciers, San Francisco (CFF)

Alliance Cat Club, Arleta (CFF)

American Burmese Association, Glendale (CFF)

California Feline Fanciers, Conago Park (CFF)

174

Frontier Allied Neuter & Spay Club, Los Angeles (CFF)

Jewel City Cat Club, Los Angeles (CFF)

American Siamese Cat Club of Japan, APO San Francisco (CFA)

Burmese Club of Southern California, Costa Mesa (CFA)

Cal-Mex All Breed Cat Club, Coronado (CFA)

California Cat Club, San Gabriel (CFA)

California Silver Fanciers, Pasadena (CFA)

California Solid Color Club, Whittier (CFA)

Camellia City Shorthair Society, Sacramento (CFA)

Camellia Solid Color Club, North Highlands (CFA)

Citrus Cat Club, Del Rosa (CFA)

Continental Cat Club, Tustin (CFA)

Crown City Cat Fanciers, Sunland (CFA)

El Camino Longhair Fanciers, Cupertino (CFA)

Emperio De San Jose Cat Fanciers, San Jose (CFA)

Fireside Cat Club, San Diego (CFA)

Fort Sutter Cat Club, Sacramento (CFA)

Franciscan Silver Fanciers, Cupertino (CFA)

Golden Gate Cat Club, San Lorenzo (CFA)

Golden West Cat Club, San Francisco (CFA)

Hacienda Cat Club, Rosmead (CFA)

Hawthorne Silver Fanciers, Van Nuys (CFA)

Imperial Russian Blue Society, Sunland, (CFA)

Inland Shorthair Society, Apple Valley (CFA)

Longhair Medley Cat Club, Temple City (CFA)

Malibu Cat Club, Pacific Palisades (CFA)

Marin County Cat Fanciers, Corte Madera (CFA)

Mt. Diablo Cat Fanciers, Lafayette (CFA)

North Bay Cat Fanciers, San Francisco (CFA)

North County Cat Club, Pacific Beach (CFA)

Northwestern Siamese Breeders, Oakland (CFA)

Old Mission Tabby & Tortie Club, Lemon Grove (CFA)

Pacific Persian Breeders, Pleasant Hill (CFA)

Pacific Tabby & Tortie Club, San Francisco (CFA)

Peninsula Cat Club, Menlo Park (CFA)

Presidio Shorthair Club, San Diego (CFA)

Riverside Cat Fanciers, Riverside (CFA)

Riverside Persian Fanciers, Riverside (CFA)

Sacramento Valley Cat Fanciers, North Highlands (CFA)

San Diego Cat Fanciers, Imperial Beach (CFA)

San Fernando Valley Cat Club, North Hollywood (CFA)

Santa Clara Valley Cat Fanciers, Cupertino (CFA)

175

Santa Monica Cat Club, Los Angeles (CFA)

Saratoga Shorthair Fanciers, San Jose (CFA)

Shorthair Society of Southern California, No. Hollywood (CFA)

Silver Cat Club of the West, San Jose (CFA)

Solid Color Club of the West (CFA), Concord

South Bay Silver Fanciers, San Pedro (CFA)

Southern California Solid Color Club, Lemon Grove (CFA)

Tabby & Tortie Club of the West, El Monte (CFA)

Town & Country Cat Club, Coronado (CFA)

Tri-County Cat Club, Belmont (CFA)

Valley Empire Cat Club, Fresno (CFA)

West Shore Cat Club, El Monte (CFA)

West Shore Shorthair Club, San Diego (CFA)

Barbary Coast Cat Fanciers, San Francisco (UCF)

Casa de Ora Cat Club, Spring Valley (UCF)

Colorpoint Shorthair Breeders, El Monte (UCF)

East Bay Cat Club, San Francisco (UCF)

Golden State Cat Club, Rosemead (UCF)

Great Western Cat Club, Los Angeles (UCF)

Havana Brown Breeders of America, Arcadia (UCF)

Lavender Foreign Sh-Breeders, San Leandro (UCF)

National Burmese Club, Sun Valley (UCF)

Orange County Sh. Cat Club, Villa Park (UCF)

Rainbow Shorthair Cat Club, So. El Monte (UCF)

Siamese Cat Soc. of California Pasadena (UCF)

Southern California Cat Club, Los Angeles (UCF)

Colorado

Colorado Cat Fanciers, Arvada (ACFA)

Connecticut

Connecticut Cat Fanciers, Bethany (CFF)

Pioneer Valley Cat Fanciers, Farmington (CFF)

Yankee Spay & Neuter Club, No. Guilford (CFF)

Nutmeg Cat Fanciers, Stamford (CFA)

Delaware

East Coast Silver Fanciers, Newark (CFA)

Eastern Tabby & Tortie Society, Newark (CFA)

Keystone Solid Color Fanciers, Newark (CFA)

District of Columbia

Cat Fanciers of Washington, Alexandria, Va. (CFA)

Florida

Venice of America Cat Club, Deerfield Beach (ACFA)

Sunshine City Cat Club, St. Petersburg (ACA)

Suncoast Cat Club, St. Petersburg (ACFA)

Circus City Cat Club, Sarasota (ACFA)

176

Platinum Coast Cat Club, Melbourne (ACFA)

Tam Bay Kittens, St. Petersburg (ACFA)

Cats of Jax, Jacksonville (CFA)

City Beautiful Cat Club, Orlando (CFA)

Gold Coast Cat Club of Florida, Ft. Lauderdale (CFA)

Manx Club of the South, St. Petersburg (CFA)

Miami Florida Cat Fanciers, North Miami (CFA)

Pelican Longhair Specialty Club, St. Petersburg (CFA)

Poinciana Shorthair Club, Miami (CFA)

Southernmost Cat Club, South Miami (CFA)

Sunland Cat Fanciers, St. Petersburg (CFA)

Florida Cat Fanciers, Tampa, (CFA)

Florida Siamese Specialty Club, Clearwater (CFA)

Florida West Coast Shorthair Breeders, St. Petersburg (CFA)

Land O'Lakes Sh Club, Tampa (ACFA)

Everglades Cat Club, Miami (CFA)

Tampi Sandi-toes Cat Club, Lutz (ACFA)

San Orlando Cat Fanciers, Winter Park (UCF)

Georgia

Crown Jewels Cat Club, Atlanta (CCFF)

Cotton States Cat Club, Winder (CFA)

Solid Color Club of the South, Atlanta (CFA)

Plantation Cat Club, Ft. Benning (ACFA)

Hawaii

Aloha Cat Club, Honolulu (CFF)

Haiku Cat Club, Kaneohe (CFF)

Diamond Head Longhair Club, Honolulu (CFA)

Hawaii All Breed Cat Club, Honolulu (CFA)

Hawaii Cat Fanciers, Honolulu (CFA)

Hawaii Shorthair Society, Honolulu (CFA)

Kailani Persian Club, Honolulu (CFA)

Royal Hawaiian Shorthair Club, Honolulu (CFA)

United Cat Fanciers of Hawaii, Honolulu (UCF)

Illinois

Greater Chicago AB Club, Libertyville (ACFA)

Lake Shore Cat Fanciers, Rolling Meadows (CCFF)

Aggregate Shorthair Cat Club, Chicago (CFA)

Archangel Society, Des Plaines (CFA)

Illinois Feline Fanciers, Springfield (CFA)

Lincoln State Cat Club, Glen Ellyn (CFA)

Mid American Persian Club, Glenview (CFA)

Windy City Shorthair Fanciers, Chicago (CFA)

Rock Valley Cat Club, Rockford (ACFA)

United Persian Society, Downers Grove (CFA)

Indiana

Summit City Cat Club, Ft. Wayne (ACFA)

Circle City Cat Club, Indianapolis (ACFA)

Carmel Cat Club, Carmel (CFF)

Hoosier Cat Fanciers, Brownsburg (CFF)

All Longhair Society, Gas City (CFA)

Chicago Shorthair Cat Club, Crown Point (CFA)

Ft. Wayne Cat Fanciers, Ft. Wayne (CFA)

Indianapolis Feline Ass'n, Indianapolis (CFA)

Michiana Cat Fanciers, South Bend (CFA)

North Shore Cat Club, Gary (CFA)

Iowa

Cat Fanciers of Iowa, Waterloo (ACFA)

Cat Fanciers of Northeast Iowa, Waterloo (CFA)

Hawkeye State Cat Club, Des Moines (CFA)

Iowa Longhair Cat Club, Des Moines (CFA)

National Shorthair Except Siamese Cat Club, Des Moines (CFA)

Kansas

Tuttle Creek Cat Club, Manhattan (ACFA)

Kentucky

Louisville Cat Club, Louisville (CCFF)

Kentuckiana Cat Club, Louisville (ACFA)

Greater Louisville Cat Breeders, Louisville (CFF)

Cincinnati Cat Club, Ft. Thomas (CFA)

National American Shorthair Society, Dayton (CFA)

Louisiana

Crescent City Cat Club, New Orleans (CCFF)

Cat Fanciers of New Orleans, Metairie (ACFA)

Bougalie Rebel's Cat Club, Westwego (CFA)

Maryland

Chesapeake Cat Club, Towson (CFA)

Massachusetts

Springfield Cat Fanciers, Springfield (CFF)

Boston Cat Club, East Bridgewater (CFA)

Solid Color Club of the East, Reading (CFA)

Shorthair Club of New England, Brockton (CFA)

Bay State Cat Fanciers, Dorchester (UCF)

Michigan

Motor City Cat Club, Lincoln Park (ACFA)

Detroit Persian Society, Highland Park (CFA)

Suburban Shorthair Society, Berkley (CFA)

Minnesota

North Star Cat Club, Mankato (ACFA)

Gopher State Cat Club, Minneapolis (ACFA)

Minnesota Siamese Cat Club, St. Paul (CFA)

Twin City Cat Fanciers, Minneapolis (CFA)

178

Twin City Solid Color Cat Club
(CFA), Minneapolis

Missouri

K.C. Midwest Cat Club, Independence (ACFA)

Ozark Empire Cat Club, Niangua (ACFA)

Central States Longhair Club, Hazelwood (CFA)

Greater St. Louis Cat Club, St. Louis (CFA)

Mo-Kan Cat Club, Kansas City (CFA)

Santa Fe Trail Shorthair Club, Kansas City (CFA)

Nebraska

Cornhusker Cat Club, Omaha (CFA)

Nevada

Glitter Gulch Cat Club, Las Vegas (CFA)

Nevada Cat Fanciers, Reno (CFA)

New Jersey

Triangle Cat Club of N.J., Rivervale (ACA)

World's Playground Jr. Feline Fanciers, Atlantic City (ACFA)

World's Playground Feline Fanciers, Atlantic City, (ACFA)

Knickerbocker Cat Club, Highland Park (CFF)

Silver Society, Audubon (CFF)

Cherry Hill Cat Club, Westmont (CFF)

American Manx Club, Denville (CFA)

Garden State Cat Club of New Jersey, Denville (CFA)

Sand & Surf Cat Club of New Jersey, Denville (CFA)

William Penn Cat Club, Trenton (CFA)

New Mexico

New Mexico Cat Fanciers, Albuquerque (CFA)

Manzano Longhair Club, Albuquerque (CFA)

Sandia Shorthair Club, Albuquerque (CFA)

New York

NTFC Cat Club, New York City (CFA)

Rochester Cat Fanciers, Rochester (ACFA)

Frontier Feline Fanciers, Hamburg (ACFA)

New England Feline Fanciers, Amawalk (CFF)

American Siamese Cat Club, New York City (CFF)

Albany Cat Fanciers, Albany (CFA)

All Shorthair Except Siamese Society, Mt. Kisco (CFA)

Colonial Cat Club, Brooklyn (CFA)

Connetquot Cat Club of Suffolk County, Elmont (CFA)

Empire Cat Club, Ossining (CFA)

Genesee Cat Fanciers' Club, Rochester (CFA)

Long Island Cat Club, Elmont (CFA)

Susquenango Cat Club, Hamilton (CFA)

Westchester Cat Club, Mt. Kisco (CFA)

Mohawk Valley Cat Fanciers, Schenectady (ACA)

Queen City Cat Club, Buffalo (ACA)

Buffalo Cat Fanciers, Williamsville (CFA)

Long Island Cat Breeders Club, Williston Park, Long Island (CFF)

Salt City Cat Club, N. Syracuse (CFA)

National Siamese Cat Club, Springfield Gardens (CFA)

U.S. Foreign Shorthair Cat Club, Mt. Kisco (CFA)

International Solid Color Society, Williamsville (CFA)

Hudson Valley Cat Fanciers, Mahopac Falls (UCF)

New York Cat Fanciers, New York City (UCF)

Ohio

Valley View Cat Club, Cleveland (CCFF)

Rubber City Cat Club, Akron (CCFF)

Buckeye Cat Club, Columbus (ACFA)

Maumee Valley Cat Club, Toledo (ACFA)

Suburban Cat Fanciers Club, Cleveland (CFF)

American Silver Fanciers, Cincinnati (CFA)

American Tabby & Tortie Club, Springfield (CFA)

Buckeye Foreign Shorthair Club, Columbus (CFA)

Cleveland Persian Society, Solon (CFA)

Cuyahoga Valley Cat Club, Akron (CFA)

Dayton Cat Fanciers, Cincinnati (CFA)

Midwest Domestic Shorthair Club, Hilliard (CFA)

Ohio State Persian Club, Hilliard (CFA)

Ohio Valley Longhair Fanciers, Cincinnati (CFA)

Western Reserve Cat Club, Youngstown (CFA)

Youngstown Cat Club, Hubbard (CFA)

Oklahoma

Oklahoma City Cat Club, Okla. City (CFA)

Oil Capital Cat Club, Tulsa (CFA)

Oklahoma Longhair Club, Okla. City (CFA)

Oklahoma Cat Club, Okla. City (ACFA)

Mustang Shorthair Fanciers, Okla. City (CFA)

Oregon

Southern Oregon Cat Club, Wolf Creek (ACFA)

Willamette Valley Cat Club, Portland (ACFA)

Santiam Cat Fanciers, Albany (ACFA)

Oregon Coast Cat Fanciers, Coquille (ACFA)

Columbia River Longhair Club, Milwaukie (CFA)

Oregon Cat Fanciers, Milwaukie (CFA)

Portland Shorthair Club, Milwaukie (CFA)

Sunset Strip Cat Fanciers, Seaside (ACFA)

Feline Fanciers of Oregon, Lake Oswego (ACFA)

Pennsylvania

Beresford Cat Club, East Lansdowne (ACA)

Eastern Cat Fanciers, Upper Darby, Del. Co. (ACA)

Great Valley Cat Club, Malvern (ACA)

Valley Forge Cat Fanciers, Trappe (ACA)

Rennaissance Cat Club, Pittsburg (CCFF)

National Domestic Shorthair Assoc., Philadelphia (CFF)

Penn State Cat Club, Roslyn (CFF)

Delaware Valley Cat Fanciers, Warminster (CFF)

Forest City Cat Club, Allison Park (CFF)

All Breed Cat Club of Washington County, Pa., Aliquippa (CFA)

Delaware Cat Fanciers, Concordville (CFA)

L&L Cat Fancier Society, Scranton (CFA)

Pittsburg Cat Club, Pittsburg (CFA)

Rhode Island

Northeast Feline Fanciers, North Scituate (CFF)

Tabby & Tortie Fanciers, Warwick (CFF)

All Breed Cat Club of the Northeast, North Kingstown (CFA)

South Carolina

Carolina Tabby & Tortie Club, Columbia (CFA)

Palmetto Cat Club, Columbia (CFA)

Tennessee

T.A.M. Cat Fanciers, Memphis (CCFF)

Memphis Cat Fanciers, Memphis (ACFA)

Bluff City Cat Club, Memphis (ACFA)

Memphis Dixieland Cat Club, Memphis (CFA)

Texas

Old Spanish Trail Cat Fanciers, Houston (CFA)

Brazos Valley Cat Club, Bryan (CCFF)

Cactus Cat Club, Ft. Worth (ACFA)

North Texas Cat Club, Richardson (ACFA)

Bayou City Cat Club, Pearland (ACFA)

Dal-Worth Shorthair Fanciers, Dallas (CFA)

Dallas Cat Club, Mesquite (CFA)

Ft. Worth Cat Fanciers, Ft. Worth (CFA)

Golden Triangle Cat Club, Kountze (CFA)

Houston Cat Club, Houston (CFA)

Silver Rebels, Houston (CFA)

Stars N'Stripes Tabby & Tortie Club, Houston (CFA)

Austin Cat Club, Austin (ACFA)

Utah

Salt Lake Cat Fanciers, Murray (CFA)

Salt Lake Longhair Club, Murray (CFA)

Salt Lake Shorthair Club, Murray (CFA)

Virginia

Old Dominion Cat Club, Richmond (CFA)

Virginia Cat Fanciers, Norfolk (CFA)

Richmond Shorthair Cat Fanciers, Richmond (CFA)

Southern Domestic & Foreign Shorthair Club, Virginia Beach (CFA)

Washington

Totem Cat Club, Tacoma (ACFA)

Cascade Cat Fanciers, Seattle (ACFA)

Seattle Cat Club, Seattle (ACFA)

Wisconsin

South Eastern Wisconsin Cat Club, Racine (ACFA)

Wisconsin Longhair Fanciers, Milwaukee (CFA)

Shorthair Cat Club of Milwaukee, Milwaukee (CFA)

Madison Cat Club, Madison (ACFA)

Milwaukee Cat Club, Milwaukee (CFA)

Canada

Canadian National Cat Club, Toronto, Ontario (ACA)

Upper Canada Cat Ass'n, Don Mills, Ontario (CCFF)

Edmonton Cat Club, Alberta (ACFA)

Victoria Cat Club, Victoria B.C. (ACFA)

Manitoba Cat Club, Winnipeg, Manitoba (ACFA)

Calgary Cat Club, Alberta (ACFA)

Cat Fanciers, Vancouver B.C. (ACFA)

Foothill Feline Fanciers, Lethbridge, Alberta (ACFA)

Calgary Canadian Cat Fancy, Alberta (CFA)

Ontario Cat Fanciers, Hamilton, Ontario (CFA)

Montreal Cat Association, Montreal P.Q. (ACA)

As in most special interest groups, the cat fancy has its own magazines. Anyone may subscribe to these leading American and foreign publications.

CATS MAGAZINE,
4 Smithfield Street,
Pittsburgh, Penna. 15222

International CAT FANCY
    Magazine,
P. O. Box 1096,
Studio City, California 91604

OUR CATS
4 Carlton Mansions,
Clapham Road,
London, S.W. 9,
England

THE CAT
29 Church Street,
Slough, Buckinghamshire,
England

THE CAT FANCY
15 Bridge Street,
Runcorn, Cheshire,
England

CATS AND KITTENS
14 Queen Street,
Derby, England

CATS MONTHLY
52 Roy Street,
Palmerston North,
New Zealand

The standard of a breed is the specification of the ideal cat of that breed, and it is the means of measuring and comparing the degrees of perfection of the various cats in the breed's competition at the cat shows. These are 1965–1966 standards of all the breeds (Chapter 5) recognized by the Cat Fanciers' Association:

PERSIAN

Color	20	Head (including size and shape of eyes, ear shape and set)	30
Coat	10		
Condition	10	Type (including shape, size, bone and length of tail)	20
Eye Color	10		

Color 20   Head (including size and shape of
Coat 10   eyes, ear shape and set) 30
Condition 10   Type (including shape, size, bone
Eye Color 10   and length of tail) 20

In all tabby varieties, the 20 points for color are to be divided 10 for markings and 10 for color.

TYPE: The perfect cat should be of cobby type—low on legs, deep in the chest, massive across the shoulders and rump, with a short and well-rounded middle piece.

SIZE: Large or medium, but no sacrifice of quality for the sake of mere size.

HEAD: Round and massive. Great breadth of skull. Well set on a neck not too long.

EARS: Small. Round tipped. Set far apart and not unduly open at the base.

NOSE: Short, snub and broad. With "break."

CHEEKS: Full.

JAWS: Broad. Powerful.

EYES: Large, round, and full. Set far apart and brilliant, giving a sweet expression to the face.

TAIL: Short. Carried without a curve and at an angle lower than the back, but not trailed, when walking.

BACK: Level.

LEGS: Thick and strong. Forelegs straight.

PAWS: Large, round and firm. Toes carried close, five in front and four behind.

COAT: Long hair, showing perfect physical condition. Of fine texture—soft, glossy and full of life. Standing off from the body. Long all over the body, including the shoulders. The ruff immense and continuing in a deep frill between the front legs. Ear tufts long and curved. Toe tufts long. Brush very full.

WITHHOLD WINNERS: Kinked or abnormal tail. Locket or Button.

Colors

WHITE: Pure white, no colored hairs. Eyes deep blue or deep copper. Odd-Eyed Whites shall have one blue and one copper eye.

BLACK: Dense coal black, sound from roots to tip of fur. Free from any tinge of rust on tips or smoke in undercoat. Eyes copper or deep orange.

BLUE: Blue color, lighter shade preferred, one level tone, without shading or marking from nose to tip of tail. Sound to the roots. Eyes copper or deep orange.

RED: Deep, rich, clear, brilliant red without shading, markings, or ticking. Lips and chin same color as coat. Eyes copper or deep orange.

CREAM: One level shade of cream, sound to the roots. Eyes copper or deep orange.

CHINCHILLA: Undercoat pure white. Coat on back, flanks, head and tail sufficiently tipped with black to give the characteristic sparkling silver appearance. Legs may be slightly shaded with tipping. Chin and ear tufts, stomach and chest pure white. Eyes green or blue-green. Rims of eyes, lips and nose outlined with black. Center of nose brick red.

SHADED SILVER: Pure, unmarked silver, with definite shading gradually down the sides, face and tail from dark on the ridge to white on chin, chest, belly, and under the tail. White undercoat. Legs the same tone as the face. The general effect to be much darker than a Chinchilla. Eyes green or blue-green. Rims of eyes, lips and nose outlined with black. Center of nose brick red.

SHELL CAMEO: Undercoat pure white. Coat on back, flanks, head and tail sufficiently tipped with red to give the char-

acteristic sparkling appearance. The face and legs may
be slightly shaded with tipping. Chin, ear tufts, stomach
and chest white. Eyes copper or deep orange. Rims of
eyes and nose leather rose.

SHADED CAMEO: Pure, unmarked red, with definite shading gradually down the sides, face and tail from dark on the
ridge to white on the chin, chest, belly and under the
tail. Legs the same tone as the face. The general effect
to be much darker than a Shell Cameo. Eyes copper or
deep orange. Rims of eyes and nose leather rose.

BLACK SMOKE: Black with white undercoat and black points and
mask. Light silver frill and ear tufts. Eyes copper or
deep orange.

BLUE SMOKE: Blue with white undercoat and blue points and
mask. White frill and ear tufts. Eyes copper or deep
orange.

CAMEO SMOKE: Red with white undercoat and red points and
mask. White frill and ear tufts. Eyes copper or deep
orange.

TABBIES

CLASSIC TABBY PATTERN: Markings dense, clearly defined, and
broad. Legs evenly barred. Bracelets coming up to meet
the body markings. Tail barred. Necklaces on neck and
chest distinct, like so many chains. Cheek swirls and
swirls on side of body, each continuing in an unbroken
ring. Marks on face, between the ears, and down the
neck, meeting the butterfly on the shoulders. The butterfly divides the head lines from the spine line. Back markings consist of a distinct stripe down the middle of the
back with stripes of the ground color on either side of it
and lines on either side of them. Lips and chin the same
shade as the rings around the eyes. Kittens and young
adults may have light chins.

MACKEREL TABBY PATTERN: Markings dense, clearly defined,
and all narrow pencillings. Legs evenly barred with

185

narrow bracelets coming up to meet the body markings. Tail barred. Necklaces on neck and chest distinct, like so many chains. Head barred with an 'M' on the forehead. Unbroken lines running back from the eyes. Lines running down the head to meet the shoulders. Spine lines run together to form a narrow saddle. Narrow pencillings run around body. Lips and chin the same shade as the rings around the eyes. Kittens and young adults may have light chins.

Colors

SILVER TABBY: Ground color pale, clear silver. Markings dense black. Eye color green or hazel.

RED TABBY: Ground color red. Markings deep, rich red. Lips and chin red. Eyes copper or deep orange.

BROWN TABBY: Ground color brilliant coppery brown. Markings dense black. Eyes copper or deep orange.

BLUE TABBY: Ground color pale bluish ivory. Markings deep blue. Lips and chin pale bluish ivory. Nose leather rose. Eyes copper or deep orange.

CREAM TABBY: Ground color pale cream. Markings darker cream. Eyes copper or deep orange.

CAMEO TABBY: Ground color pale cream. Markings red. Eyes copper or deep orange.

❋   ❋   ❋   ❋   ❋   ❋   ❋

TORTOISESHELL: Unbrindled patches of black, red, and cream. Patches bright, clearly defined, and well broken, even to the feet. Part of the face black, part red, known as the "Blaze." Eyes copper or deep orange.

CALICO: Unbrindled patches of black, red, and cream, interspersed with white. Patches bright, clearly defined. White in distinct, predominant areas on chest, face, legs and paws. White Blaze. Eyes copper or deep orange.

BLUE-CREAM: Unbrindled patches of blue and cream. Patches bright, clearly defined and well broken, even to the feet. Eyes copper or deep orange.

❋   ❋   ❋   ❋   ❋   ❋   ❋

PEKE-FACE RED AND RED TABBY: The Peke-Face cat should conform in color, markings and general type to the standards set forth for the red and red tabby Persian cat. The head should resemble as much as possible that of the Pekingese dog from which it gets its name. Nose should be very short and depressed, or indented between the eyes. There should be a decidedly wrinkled muzzle. Eyes round, large and full, set wide apart, prominent and brilliant.

HIMALAYAN

Color	20	Head (including size and shape of eyes, ear shape and set)	30
Coat	10		
Condition	10	Type (including shape, size, bone and length of tail)	20
Eye Color	10		

The 20 points for color are to be divided 10 for body color and 10 for points.

TYPE: Same as for Persians.

COLOR AND POINTS: Same as for Siamese with the following color classes:

CHOCOLATE, SEAL, LILAC, AND BLUE POINT: Same as for Siamese.

FLAME POINT: Body creamy white. Points a delicate orange flame, free of barring and uniform in color.

EYES: Blue.

WITHHOLD WINNERS: Kinked Tail, Crossed Eyes, White Toes.

ABYSSINIAN

Color and Ticking	30	Eyes	10
Type-Body and Tail	25	Coat	10
Head and Ears	20	Condition	5

BODY AND TAIL: Body medium long, lithe and graceful but showing well developed muscular strength. Legs proportionately slim, fine boned, with feet small, round, neat and compact. When standing giving the impression of being on tip-toe. Tail thick at base, fairly long and tapering. Tipped with black or brown. Abyssinian conformation strikes a medium between the extremes of the cobby and the svelte, lengthy type. General balance more to be desired than mere size.

HEAD AND EARS: Head a modified, slightly rounded wedge without flat planes; the brow, cheek and profile lines all showing a gentle contour. A slight rise from the bridge of the nose to the forehead. Forehead of good size with width between the ears and flowing into the arched neck without a break. Muzzle not sharply pointed. Allowance to be made for jowls in the males. Ears alert, large, and pointed—broad at base, preferably tipped with black or brown. Hair on ears very short and close-lying. Inner ear bare and open.

EYES: Almond shaped, large, brilliant and expressive. Skull aperture follows almond shape of eyes—neither round nor Oriental. Color, amber or green, the more richness and depth the better.

COAT: Soft, silky, fine in texture, but dense and resilient to the touch, with a lustrous sheen. Medium in length but long enough to accommodate two or three bands of ticking separated by lighter bands.

CONDITION: Lithe, hard and muscular, giving the appearance of activity, sound health, and general vigor.

WITHHOLD WINNERS: Kinked or abnormal tail.

DISQUALIFY: Black pads or any black hair on the Red Abyssinian.

Colors

RUDDY: Ruddy brown, ticked with various shades of darker brown or black. Darker shading along spine allowed if fully ticked. The underside and forelegs (inside) to be a tint to harmonize with the main body color; undersides and inside of forelegs to show no more ticking than a single band of darker color at the tip of a hair, preference given to unmarked orange-brown (burnt sienna) color. Nose leather tile red. Nostril, chin and upper throat area white or reddish cream. Paw pads black with black extending beyond the paws of the hind legs. Evenly ticked with double or triple bands of color on each hair over saddle, sides, chest and tail, without patching or irregularity.

Color: 15 points. Ticking: 15 points.

RED: Warm glowing red, distinctly ticked with chocolate-brown. Deeper shades of red preferred. Ears and tail tipped with chocolate-brown. Paw pads pink, with chocolate-brown between toes extending beyond the paws of the hind legs. Nose leather rosy pink. Body color on kittens usually lighter.

SIAMESE

Color	25	Head (including ear set)	20
Coat	10	Type (including shape, size and svelteness)	20
Condition	5	Color and shape of eyes	20

HEAD: Long and tapering in a fine wedge from ears to narrow muzzle, with no whisker break. The receding chin caused by failure of the upper and lower teeth to meet in a straight line shall be considered a serious fault. Skull flat. Nose a continuation of the forehead with no break. In profile a straight line is seen from the center of the forehead to the tip of the nose. Allowance for jowls in a stud cat. Ears large and pricked, wide at base, and continuing the line of the wedge. Long flat profile, 6; Fine muzzle, 4; chin, 4; width between eyes, 2; ears, 4.

BODY: Medium in size, dainty, long and svelte. Neck long and slender. Legs proportionately long and slim. Hind legs higher than the front. Feet small and oval. Tail long and tapering. Body, 7; Neck, 4; Legs and Feet, 5; Tail, 4.

EYES: Almond in shape and slanting toward nose in true Oriental fashion. Color, 10 (clear, 5; deep blue, 5); Shape, 10 (Oriental, 5; not crossed, 5).

COAT: Short, fine in texture, glossy, lying close to the body. Short Coat, 3; Fine coat, 2; Glossy coat, 2; Close coat, 3.

COLOR: In older cats, allowance should be made for darker coats, as Siamese generally darken with age, but there should be a definite contrast between body color and points. Proper color, 4; shading, 4; evenness of color, 7.

POINTS: Mask, ears, legs, feet and tail, dense and clearly defined. All of the same shade. Mask should be connected to the ears by tracings. Mask, 2; Ears, 2; Legs, 2; Feet, 2; Tail 2.

CONDITION: Good physical condition. Inclined to muscle. Not fat.

WITHHOLD WINNERS: A definite visible misplacement of any joint in the tail. White toes. Locket or button.

Colors

SEAL POINT: Body even pale fawn to cream, shading gradually into a lighter color on the stomach and chest. Points deep seal brown. Eyes clear and vivid deep blue. Foot pads and nose leather the same color as the points.

BLUE POINT: Body bluish-white shading gradually to an oyster white on the stomach and chest. Points blue. Eyes clear and deep blue. Foot pads and nose leather slate colored.

CHOCOLATE POINT: Body ivory. Points milk chocolate color. Eyes clear and deep blue. Foot pads and nose leather cinnamon pink.

LILAC POINT: Body glacial white. Points frosty grey with pinkish tone. Eyes clear and deep blue. Foot pads and nose leather mauve.

BURMESE

Color	25	Eyes	10
Head and Ears	25	Coat	10
Body and Tail	25	Condition	5

The overall impression of the ideal Burmese would be a cat of medium size and rich solid color; with substantial bone structure, good muscular development and a surprising weight for its size. This, together with its expressive eyes and sweet face, presents a totally distinctive cat which is comparable to no other breed.

COLOR: The mature specimen should be rich, warm sable brown; shading almost imperceptibly to a slightly lighter hue on the underparts, but otherwise without shadings or markings of any kind. Allowance should be made for lighter color and possible faint striping in adolescents and kittens.

BODY AND TAIL: Body medium in size, muscular in development, and presenting a somewhat compact appearance. Allowance to be made for larger size in males. An ample, rounded chest, with back level from shoulder to tail. Legs well proportioned to body, with round feet. Tail straight, medium in length. Body, 15; Legs and Feet, 5; Tail, 5.

HEAD AND EARS: The head should be pleasingly rounded without flat planes whether viewed from front or side. Face should be full, with considerable breadth between the eyes, tapering slightly to a short, well developed muzzle. In profile there should be a visible nose break. Ears to be medium in size and set well apart on a rounded skull; alert, tilting slightly forward, broad at base with slightly rounded tips. Roundness of head, 7; full face with proper profile, 8; breadth between eyes, 4; ear set and placement, 6.

EYES: Set far apart and with rounded aperture, with color ranging from yellow to gold, the greater the depth and brilliance the better. Green eyes a fault. Blue eyes to disqualify. Placement and shape, 5; Color, 5.

COAT: Fine, glossy, satin-like in texture; very close lying. Short, 4; Texture, 4; Close-lying, 2.

CONDITION: Perfect physical condition, with excellent muscle tone. There should be no evidence of obesity, paunchiness, weakness or apathy.

WITHHOLD WINNERS: Kinked or abnormal tail. Locket or button.
DISQUALIFY: Blue eyes.

AMERICAN SHORTHAIR

Color	20	Head (including size and shape of eyes, ear shape and set)	30
Coat	10		
Condition	10	Type (including shape, size, bone and length of tail)	20
Eye Color	10		

In all tabby varieties, the 20 points for color are to be divided 10 for markings and 10 for color.

HEAD: Broad, with cheeks especially well developed in studs. Nose and face medium short with eyes set wide apart. Muzzle presenting a squarish aspect but should not be as short as in the Persians.

EARS: Medium in size, rounded at tips, wide set and not too large at base.

EYES: Round, full, set to show breadth of nose.

CHIN: Well developed, forming a perpendicular line with the upper lip.

NECK: Medium short and denoting strength, and in proportion to the body.

BODY: Well knit and powerful, showing good depth, full chest, and ranging from medium to large in size.

TAIL: Slightly heavy at base, tapering to an abrupt end and in proportion to the body.

LEGS AND FEET: Legs of good substance and in proportion to the body. Not too high on legs. Feet neat and well rounded.

COAT: Short, thick, even in texture, well bodied giving a general appearance of shortness. Somewhat heavier and thicker during winter months.

COLOR: Requirements for color of coat and eye color are the same as for Persians.

CONDITION: Hard and muscular, giving a general appearance of strength and vigor.

BALANCE: All physical aspects of the cat should complement each other to present a perfect picture.

WITHHOLD WINNERS: Kinked or abnormal tail. Locket or button.

HAVANA BROWN

Head	15	Coat	15
Whiskers	5	Color	15
Eyes	10	Legs	10
Ears	5	Tail	5
Body and Neck	15	Condition	5

HEAD: Longer than it is wide, with a distinct stop at the eyes. Narrowing to a rounded muzzle with a slight break behind the whiskers. Allowance for stud jowls and sparse furnishings on the lower lip.

WHISKERS: Brown.

EARS: Large, round-tipped, with very little hair inside or out. Wide-set but not flaring.

EYES: Chartreuse green, the greener shades preferred. Oval in shape.

BODY AND NECK: Body medium in length, firm and muscular. Neck proportioned to the body.

LEGS: Proportioned to the body. Paws oval.

TAIL: Medium in length. In proportion to the body.

COAT: Medium in length. Smooth.

COLOR: Rich, warm, mahogany brown. Entire coat should be the same sound shade of brown to the skin. Nose leather and paw pads have a rosy tone.

CONDITION: Firm and muscular. Coat glossy. Eyes clear.

WITHHOLD WINNERS: Kinked or abnormal tail. Locket or button.

MANX

Color and Markings	5	Shortness of Back	5
Coat	15	Legs and Feet	15
Body	25	Head and Ears	10
Depth of Flank	5	Eyes	5
Taillessness	10	Condition	5

COLOR AND MARKINGS: All colors of Manx are recognized.

COAT: Short, of good texture, with a well padded quality arising from the longer outer coat and the thicker undercoat, known as a "double coat."

BODY: Solid, compact, and well balanced, with the back showing a definite incline from the shoulders to the haunches. Small or medium in size. "Bunnylike" in appearance.

DEPTH OF FLANK: Of great depth, adding to the cobbiness and balance.

TAILLESSNESS: Absolute in a perfect specimen. A decided hollow at the end of the backbone where, in the ordinary cat, a tail would begin.

SHORTNESS OF BACK: Back should be sturdy and short, so as to conform with the actual size of the well balanced cat.

LEGS AND FEET: Legs of good substance, with front legs short and well set apart to show good depth of chest. Back legs much longer with a heavy, muscular thigh tapering to a substantial lower leg that often has the hair worn off due to the fact that the Manx rests on this part as often as on the paws. Feet small, neat and well rounded with five toes in front and four toes on the back legs.

HEAD AND EARS: Head fairly round with prominent cheeks and a jowly appearance. Muzzle tapering but not to a sharp point. Head medium in length without a definite nose break. Ears rather wide at base, tapering slightly to a point and longer than those of the Domestic, but in proportion to the head.

EYES: Large, round, and full. Color standard according to color of coat as in other breeds. Points to be divided equally between size and color.

CONDITION: Good physical condition. Muscular, good flesh, but not fat.

PENALIZE: A rise of the bone at the end of the spine. A nonvisible joint or cartilage.

WITHHOLD WINNERS: Definite, visible tail joint.

RUSSIAN BLUE

Color	20	Eye Color	5
Coat	25	Eye Shape	5
Body and Tail	15	Ears	5
Head and Neck	20	Condition	5

COLOR: Clear blue. Even throughout, and in maturity free from tabby markings or shading. Lighter or lavender blue preferred.

COAT: Short, thick and very fine. Standing up soft and silky like sealskin. Very different fur from that of any other breed. The coat is double so that it has a distinct silvery sheen. The texture and appearance of the coat is the truest criterion of the Russian Blue.

BODY AND TAIL: Body long; lithe and graceful outline and carriage. Fine in bone. Tail fairly long and tapering. Legs long. Feet small, and oval.

HEAD AND NECK: Skull flat and long. Face appearing broad across the eyes because of the heavy fur. Nose, medium in length. Neck long but appearing short because of the heavy fur.

EYES: Set wide apart. Almond in shape. In maturity, vivid green.

EARS: Medium in size. Wide at base. Pointed at the tips and with very little inside fur. Skin of ears thin and not too thickly covered with hair.

WITHHOLD WINNERS: Kinked or abnormal tail. Locket or button.

RED COLORPOINT

The Red Colorpoint Shorthair is a separate breed. The type description and scale of points is the same as for the Siamese. Body color clear white with any shading in the same tone as the points. Points dense, deep red with all points matching.

REX

Head	10	Legs	5
Neck	5	Coat	30
Ears	5	Color	10
Eyes	5	Condition	5
Tail	5	Balance	5
Body	15		

HEAD: Longer than it is wide with a break at the muzzle when viewed from the front. A Roman profile. A straight line from the top of the nose to the chin. Shape and muzzle break, 5; Profile, 3; Chin, 2.

NECK: Long and slender.

EARS: Large and naked. Set high on head. Taller than they are wide with a modified point at the tip.

EYES: Medium in size. Oval in shape. Color in keeping with the coat color is desirable but secondary to the overall appearance of the eyes.

TAIL: Long and slender. Tapering slightly from the body to the end. Sometimes tipped with a tuft of waves. No penalty for a bare upper surface.

BODY: Long, slender, with "tuck-up" behind the ribs. Hips heavy in proportion to the rest of the body. Hard and muscular. Medium to small in size with fine bone. Body, 10; Tuck-Up, 5.

LEGS: Long and slender in keeping with type of body and tail. High on the legs with feet that are dainty.

COAT: Fine, soft, short, and dense. A deep even wave is desirable, especially on the back and tail. Coat on head and legs the texture of velvet pile. Texture, 10; Density, 10; Waviness, 10.

COLOR: All colors of Rex are recognized.

CONDITION: Firm and muscular. Lack of condition shows in flabbiness, loss of coat quality and dullness in the eyes. Disposition calm.

BALANCE: Viewed as a whole, the cat shall be well knit, smooth, and each part in good proportion.

WITHHOLD WINNERS: Kinked or abnormal tail.

DISQUALIFY: Any coarse or guard hairs.

The cat fancy regards the winner of the Cat of the Year title as the national champion, but actually the winner is an international champion, for Canadian cats are also included in the competition. But whether he (or she) is United States champion or international champion, or even North American champion, he is certainly the supreme cat on this side of the Atlantic and has no other worlds to conquer. The annual award was established by *Cats Magazine* in 1947 and has been continued ever since then. The system rates all purebred cats in competition at official cat shows in this country and Canada.

The record of selections for Cat of the Year and Cat of the Year, Opposite Sex:

Cat of the Year		*Opposite Sex*
Wimauma Masterpiece of Chalsu Blue Persian, m Charles Victor	1947	Vee Roi's Lantara Gene Blue point Siamese, f Mrs. R. H. Hecht
Dixie-Land's Pearl Harbor Yank Blue Parsian, m Mrs. J. H. Revington	1948	Vee Roi's Katisha Seal point Siamese, f Mrs. R. H. Hecht
Dixi-Land's Felice of Nor-mont Blue Persian, f Maurine Hoag	1949	Dixi-Land's White Historian II Copper-eyed, white Persian, m Mrs. J. H. Revington
Lavender Liberty Beau Blue Persian, m Anthony De-Santis	1950	Vee Roi's Lantara Gene Blue point, Siamese, f Mrs. R. H. Hecht
Pied Piper of Barbe Bleue Black Persian, m Bess A. Morse & Frances Campbell	1951	Rosedere DeAnne of Nor-mont Blue-cream, Persian, f Maurine Hoag
Great Lakes Timothy of Rosemont Blue Persian, m Frances Kosierowski	1952	Cymri Dee-Va. Seal point, Siamese, f Lillian Pedulla
Arlington's Sensation II Chinchilla, Persian, f Maurine Hoag	1953	Moonbeam of Gaylands Blue Persian, m Verner Clum
Kerry Lu Ramon of Casa Contenta Chinchilla, Persian, m Dr. & Mrs. V. Van Zele	1954	Ammon Ra's Taisho Seal point, Siamese, f Lillian Magner
Kerry Lu Ramon of Casa Contenta Chinchilla, Persian, m Dr. & Mrs. V. Van Zele	1955	Flagstone's Play Girl Shaded Silver Persian, f Helen Mueller
Tempura Yours Truly Blue point, Siamese, m Mr. & Mrs. Richard Birkett	1956	La Chatta of Beverly-Serrano Chinchilla, Persian, f Mr. & Mrs. L. H. Peterson
Dixi-Land's Sir Gai of Nor-mont Blue Persian, m Maurine Hoag	1957	Nor-mont's Silver Jewell Chinchilla, Persian, f Maurine Hoag
Rosemont Golden Boy Cream Persian, m Frances Kosierowski	1958	Wolfgang Melody of Be-Ba Seal point, Siamese, f E. T. Baker
Vel-Vene's Voodoo Black Persian, m Robert A. Green	1959	Career Girl of Nor-mont Blue Persian, f Maurine Hoag

197

Cat of the Year		*Opposite Sex*
Shawnee Moonflight Copper-eyed, White Persian, m Nikki Horner Shuttleworth	1960	Shawnee Soap Suds Copper-eyed, White Persian, f Nikki Horner Shuttleworth
Shawnee Moonflight Copper-eyed, White Persian, m Nikki Horner Shuttleworth	1961	Windibank Patti-Kake of Azulita Copper-eyed, White Persian, f Mrs. Walker K. Johnston
Chez Moumette Cal of Nor-mont Cream Persian, m Maurine Hoag	1962	Wolfgang Liebsti II of Thani Blue point, Siamese, f Noel & Helen Arthur
Azulita Pale-face of Casa Cielo Copper-eyed, White Persian, m Mrs. Walker K. Johnston	1963	Nor-mont Confection Blue Persian, f Maurine Hoag
Shawnee Moonflight Copper-eyed, White Persian, m Nikki Horner Shuttleworth	1964	Shawnee White Wash Copper-eyed, White Persian, f Nikki Horner Shuttleworth
Shawnee Trademark Silver Tabby American Shorthair, m Nikki Horner Shuttleworth	1965	Shawnee White Wash Copper-eyed, White Persian, f Nikki Horner Shuttleworth

Here is some of the material that has contributed to my knowledge of cats, and information harvested from their pages will be found throughout the pages of this book. I recommend these to all admirers of cats.

Aberconway, Christabel. A DICTIONARY OF CAT LOVERS. Michael Joseph, Ltd., London, 1949.

Bryant, Doris. PET CATS, Their Care and Handling. Ives Washburn, Inc., New York, 1963.

Budge, Sir Ernest A. Wallis. THE BOOK OF THE DEAD. University Books, Inc., New Hyde Park, New York, 1960.

Carr, William H. A. THE BASIC BOOK OF THE CAT. Charles Scribner's Sons, New York, 1963.

Crawford, Nelson A. CATS IN PROSE AND VERSE. Coward-McCann, Inc., New York, 1947.

CFA YEAR BOOKS. 1958, 1959, editor, Mrs. Joan Van Zele. 1960, 1961, editor, Mrs. A. M. Dickie. 1962, 1963, 1964, 1965, editor, Mrs. Christine Streetman. CFA Central Office, 39 East Front Street, Red Bank, N.J.

Droscher, Vitus B., translated by Huggard, Eveleen. THE MYSTERIOUS SENSES OF ANIMALS. E. P. Dutton & Co., Inc., New York, 1965.

Jude, A. C. CAT GENETICS. All-Pets Books, now T. F. H. Publications, Jersey City, 1955.

Martin, Ethel Austin. NUTRITION IN ACTION. Holt, Rinehart & Winston, Inc., New York, 1963.

Pond, Grace. THE OBSERVER'S BOOK OF THE CAT. Frederick Warne & Co., Ltd., New York and London, 1959.

Ramsdale, Jeanne. PERSIAN CATS AND OTHER LONGHAIRS. T. F. H. Publications, Inc., Jersey City, 1964.

Reighard, Jacob and Jennings, H. S., 3rd edition by Elliot, Rush. ANATOMY OF THE CAT. Henry Holt & Co., New York, 1935.

Scott, W. S. A CLOWDER OF CATS. John Westhouse, Ltd., London, 1946.

Simpson, Frances. THE BOOK OF THE CAT. Cassell & Co., Ltd., London, Paris, New York, Melbourne, 1903.

Van Vechten, Carl. THE TIGER IN THE HOUSE. Alfred A. Knopf, Inc., New York, 1936, fifth printing 1960.

Walker, Ernest P. MAMMALS OF THE WORLD. The Johns Hopkins Press, Baltimore, 1964.

Whitney, Leon F. THE COMPLETE BOOK OF CAT CARE, Doubleday and Co., New York, 1953.

Winslow, Helen M. CONCERNING CATS. Lothrop Publishing Co., Boston, 1900.

Wolfgang, Harriet. SHORTHAIRED CATS. T. F. H. Publications, Inc., Jersey City, 1963.

Index